INSIDE
WORLD
RELIGIONS

AN ILLUSTRATED GUIDE

Kevin O'Donnell

Fortress Press
Minneapolis

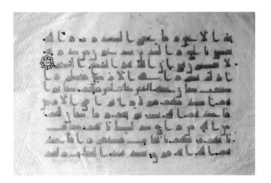

INSIDE WORLD RELIGIONS
An Illustrated Guide

First Fortress Press edition 2007

Published in collaboration with LionHudson, Oxford.

Cover image: Goran Tomasevic/Reuters/Corbis UK Ltd.

Library of Congress Cataloging-in-Publication Data
O'Donnell, Kevin, 1957 Feb. 3-
  Inside world religions : an illustrated guide
  / Kevin O'Donnell.
     p. cm.
  ISBN-13: 978-0-8006-3889-4 (alk. paper)
  ISBN-10: 0-8006-3889-1 (alk. paper)
  1. Religions. I. Title.
  BL80.3.O36 2006
  200—dc22
                    2006028646

Printed and bound in China.

Contents

Introduction

'"Curiouser and curiouser!" cried Alice (she was so much surprised, that for the moment, she quite forgot how to speak good English); "now I'm opening out like the largest telescope that ever was!"'

Lewis Carroll, *Alice in Wonderland*

A book about world faiths might attract many kinds of readers, from the open-minded seeker to the ardent believer of a particular creed who wishes to understand others in order to denounce their errors. There are many positions in between. However we come to the topic, there will be an opening up, a mental expansion, a greater awareness of the great traditions of the

world's faiths, whatever we might end up making of them. I have written this book as a committed Christian, yet I have tried to write in as balanced and as neutral a fashion as I can, presenting the facts and letting each faith speak honestly for itself. No doubt I have failed in that aim at times, as the task is humanly impossible. We can never free ourselves of our unconscious subtexts and prejudices, no matter how we try, whether we are believers, atheists or agnostics. I have tried to be fair, honest and as thorough as possible. This book is designed as a taster, somewhere between a pocket guide and an academic tome.

As a Christian, I can honestly say that I have also found much of interest and value in other faiths, and while I cannot advocate blending them together into a religious soup of relativism, there is much of value that we can learn from each other's beliefs, even when we might disagree strongly on other matters.

Studying other faiths encourages dialogue and cooperation without necessarily compromising one's own precious beliefs. It can affirm and confirm those beliefs too, either when they are attested as something common to many faiths, or, conversely, when they are found to be unique, missing from other creeds. They are then precious jewels indeed. Studying other faiths also emphasizes the common spiritual quest that we can trace right through human history, and this echoes the words of Augustine of Hippo: 'Our hearts are restless, O God, until we find our rest in Thee.'

WHAT IS A RELIGION?

How do we define a religion? There are many starting points and angles to approach this from. A religion is a social fact with its own historical development in a specific social and economic situation. It is also a guide and a treasure for those inside the faith in question. Many might be the insights and experiences that the adherents of a particular religion claim and enjoy.

Attempts to study religions took on structure and a rational framework in the nineteenth century. Before this, the Enlightenment philosophers had poured scorn on the supernatural, and earlier still, the world faiths had sought to understand each other either in order to condemn each other or to blend and create a new movement (thus Sikhism arose from a meeting of Islam and Hinduism).

The pioneering work of the German scholar Friedrich Max Müller led to the creation of the first university professorships of religious studies in the last quarter of the nineteenth century. The Dutch scholar Pierre Daniel Chantepie de Saussaye developed a cataloguing approach to religions, describing artefacts, rituals and key beliefs, rather like a handbook on botany might describe plants. Ninian Smart and Mircea Eliade, working in the late twentieth century, catalogued in this way, describing symbols and rituals, higher and more primitive religious belief, the prophetic and the mystical. The problem was that these approaches did not always do justice to religion as a living organism. A faith is filled with believers who have hopes, fears and blessings. The cataloguing approach has limitations in botany too. Dissecting a plant and setting out all the pieces is a meticulous, precise and informative process and it can teach you a great deal about a plant. However, something is missing: the living, growing nature of the plant when it was unplucked and entire, *in situ* and in context. Something similar is true with religion. Ninian Smart recognized this lack and eventually developed his ideas to include an all-important experiential dimension.

AVOIDING BIAS

The philosophy of Edmund Husserl (1859–1938) came to the aid of the students of religion. He put forward the idea that we could only confidently speak about what was in our conscious experience from interaction with the world. In this phenomenological approach, when studying religions as historical and social phenomena, we have to be aware of our own feelings, prejudices and the effect that our study has upon us. There must be a ruthless attempt to shun such prejudice, and yet, in a Zen-like act of irony and humility, we have to admit that it is always with us. We need to 'bracket out' our own beliefs and values when studying another's. We need to try to have empathy with the feelings of others and we need to foster our imaginations to see the thrust, the sense, the spirit behind a movement. We must also listen to the views of the insiders, and if their evaluation of their faith is different from ours, we must ask who can claim to be right.

All of this took the cataloguing or listing of phenomena a stage further, admitting the difficulties of neutrality and the problem of reaching the same vision as the insider.

The scholar Gavin Flood, in *Beyond Phenomenology*, recently argued that we need to take more seriously the context of each faith: socially, historically and within the experiential world of the believing insider. He appeals for a strong 'metatheory', a discipline that criticizes our underlying assumptions about what we are studying. Thus, the academics can agree upon one thing: studying religions is akin to juggling. You have to keep the balls of your own values and beliefs in the air along with those of another.

EVOLUTIONARY DILEMMAS

The end of the nineteenth century saw the huge impact of Darwin's theories. Anthropologists worked with this framework, assuming that there must be a steady advance from the primitive and superstitious to the rational and civilized (assuming this to be Western civilization). Sir James Frazer followed this model for his research on primal religion in *The Golden Bough* (1890–1915, with the abridged edition published in 1922). He saw three distinct ages coming into play, those of Magic, Religion and Science. Primal religion belonged to the first, the great world faiths to the second, and the age of the Enlightenment to the last. He did admit, though, in a rare moment of honest humility, that the third age might not be the final word. This might be superseded by yet another age at some point in the future that we could not possibly understand now. Perhaps we are seeing something of this in modern society as a synthesis is attempted between the technological, the ethical and the spiritual, with the rise of the New Age Movement and various New Religious Movements (NRMs) being

worshipping and ethical, is the joy of being human.

Fraser's work was criticized by later students of religion as being too armchair-based. They would now stress the need to get out into the field, *in situ*, and see how rituals and beliefs work for real people. They speak of 'participant observation' and the need for religions to be able to speak for themselves. The voice of the interpreter, and the colouring of his or her prejudices, is acknowledged.

Primal religion, too, was not all superstition and sympathetic magic. These elements were there, as people thought that fire was a spirit rising or that water moved because it had a god within it. Animism and magical potions, rituals and sacrifices were a part of early humanity. There was also awe and wonder at life and the world, and a strong sense of community and obligation. This can be seen in studies of the rainforest tribes of the Amazon today, with their sense of respect for nature, for keeping balance and for enjoying a simple but fulfilling lifestyle that is subsistence based. There is also much that is unknown about early religion though, because nothing was written down.

Sir James Fraser, author of The Golden Bough

created. The present generation seems more open to the spiritual, the mystical and that which cannot be quantified.

Postmodernism allows far more space for the intuitive and the symbolic to play, rejecting the judgement of everything by reason alone. Truth can be seen in many forms, in the arts and the poetic as well as in scientific method. Indeed, the early twentieth-century philosopher Ludwig Wittgenstein denounced the rationalism of Fraser for reducing religion by explanation. He compared the power of religion to that of music. You cannot explain either; you experience them and they move you. His idea of language games helped to set out the postmodern stall of many disciplines and overlapping ideas; reason does not call all the shots. To be poetic and emotional, to be

IN THE BEGINNING, ONE GOD?

There is a debate about belief in one God only, monotheism, being the original form of religion. This was long assumed by Jews, Christians and Muslims the world over, following the story of creation and the first man and woman, Adam and Eve. Paul, following this lead, argued that belief in many gods, polytheism, was a degeneration, a result of hardening hearts as people turned away from the living God (see Romans 1:21–23).

This view was rejected by scholars working with an evolutionary perspective in the nineteenth and twentieth centuries. They assumed that monotheism was a more elevated, sophisticated theology that slowly developed in various parts of the world. They saw a long haul in the pages of the Hebrew Scriptures, for example, from patriarchs who followed clan deities such as the Canaanite god El to the monolatry of Moses (he may have assumed other gods existed, but the Hebrews were bound to worship Yahweh alone). True monotheism may only have come with the great prophets of the sixth century BCE, such as Isaiah. They stated, unequivocally, that there was only one God, and no others. Other tribes and peoples slowly displaced their pantheon of gods in favour of their chief deity or High God, and so, for example, Zeus became for later, more philosophical Greeks simply 'God'.

This is possible, though others speculate that the very existence of High Gods in primal religion suggests an awareness of an original worship of that Being alone in a special way, with various other spirit beings in attendance. Wilhelm Schmidt presented such a hypothesis in 1912 with *The Origin of the Idea of God*. He appealed to the remoteness of the High God (often the Sky God) in primal religions and his lack of an earthly cult. Lesser deities tied to the earth, such as fire and water spirits, were more approachable and had their cults, offerings and priesthoods. The remote High God was an echo of the early monotheism before hardness of heart set in. Schmidt was swimming very much against the tide in the early twentieth century, but with contemporary questioning of the evolutionary mindset and agenda, his approach can be looked at afresh. Recent researches that might reveal an original monotheism in ancient China also add grist to the mill.

Originally, the High God may have been perceived as the Fount of all life, including any other deities, spirits or angels. If there were such an original vision, then any definitive evidence of it across the world has been lost or lies undiscovered; further researches might develop this hypothesis more robustly. One can only point to the varied testimony to High Gods and occasional prayers and hymns that seek them out as the Real Thing, the Big Truth, such as some material in the earliest scriptures of Hinduism, the *Rg Veda*. There we might have a glimpse of some form of original monotheism with a Big God. If we recall the revision of evolutionary schemes, admitting that what was early could contain wisdom and the sublime, and that not all that comes later is necessarily more advanced, we have to leave this one as an open question.

Wherever we started, we have arrived here today. Behind most modern faiths there is a transcendent reality, the Other, a Mystery.

COMMON VISION

Attempts are made to cross-reference religions and to draw together common threads and vision. Aldous Huxley attempted this in the early twentieth century with his appeal to a perennial philosophy, a wisdom of the ancients that burns and throbs at the heart of all people and in all faiths. It is an intoxicating idea, but beyond a common search for God, a belief in an unseen, transcendent reality, a hope of immortality and some very basic ethics, any attempt to delineate such a perennial philosophy soon dissipates like the mirage that it is. The details of world faiths and their beliefs are often contradictory as well as convergent.

More helpfully, Rudolf Otto urged the idea of the numinous upon us in his *Idea of the Holy* in 1917. He spoke of experience of the divine as a *mysterium tremendum et fascinans*, a mystery that both makes us weak at the knees and fascinates us, draws us. This was the experience of the numinous, whether that of a Neolithic tribesman approaching the inner sanctum of a cave by torchlight, an Egyptian priest making offerings for Pharaoh, or a Catholic priest at the mass. Religion has that power and that pull. It touches deep things, and God, as the theologian Paul Tillich once said, is really about 'Ultimate Concern' and 'the Ground of our Being'.

In everyday life, this is the awe found in the face of the sunset, or the sense of a presence felt by a poet like Wordsworth while rowing in the English Lake District. In children's fiction, it is the vision found by Rat and Mole:

'Breathless and transfixed the Mole stopped rowing as the liquid run of that glad piping broke on him like a wave, caught him up, and possessed him utterly. He saw the tears on his comrade's cheeks, and bowed his head and understood.'

Kenneth Grahame
The Wind in the Willows

The realm of religious experience is a rich and fertile ground for study. The first serious work on this was published in the early twentieth century by William James in *The Varieties of Religious Experience*. James was concerned with psychology and the consciousness. He collected many testimonies and stories from people and analysed the data. He outlined two basic religious types: that of the optimist who had a heart-warming experience, and the pessimist who felt a burden of sin. Religious conversion he saw as a psychodynamic, a way of resolving tensions in the psyche.

James's work was followed up by more careful collections of data by teams of people. These reveal widespread belief in religious experience. In the USA, for example, surveys have revealed that about 15 per cent of people responded with stories of Near Death Experiences. About a third responded positively to the question, 'Have you felt as though you were close to a powerful spiritual force that seemed to lift you out of yourself?' The replies were by no means always from people involved in institutional religion. These surveys and results have been replicated elsewhere. Research in Nottingham, England, for example, in 1981 revealed that just over 50 per cent gave a positive response. The responses could be from any social class, although there was a higher proportion of women. Experiences could be as a result of a crisis, or of awe in religious worship, or of wonder at the beauty of nature.

Apart from the widespread existence of such experiences, research from James onwards attests that people do not only turn to God in a crisis, which is often the claim of the sceptic, but also as a response to sheer mystery, awe and beauty.

Members of world faiths often claim experiences, answered prayers, healings and visions today. A number of Christians claim to be able to 'speak in tongues', praising God in a language they do not understand. Researchers have shown that these people are calm and balanced and whatever the phenomenon is, it is far from being neurotic in origin.

SEEKING COMMON GROUND

There are convergences. There is a common search and common values. One should not be surprised at this. As a Christian, I will make appeal to the notion of being made 'in the image of God' as a thinking, feeling, spiritual being who can sense and search for the divine. A Buddhist might appeal to the nature of the eternal *Dharma* (the Way or Truth) and the Buddha nature within all living beings. Each person can tune into this enlightenment. A Hindu or a Sikh might appeal to the belief that we carry the *atman* within, a spark of the divine that lies deep within all living things. There are different ideas, different terms, some contradictory understandings, but some common ground. There is something in humans that can appreciate the eternal and the ethical.

There are many such overlapping values and it is intriguing that many faiths have their own version of the Golden Rule set out by Jesus:

'Do for others what you want them to do for you.'

Jesus

'That which you hate do not do to your neighbour.'

Rabbi Hillel

'What you do not wish done to yourself, do not to others.'

Confucius

'Let none of you treat your brother in a way he himself would dislike to be treated.'

Qur'an

'Do not do to another what you would not like to be done to yourself; that is the gist of the law…'

Mahabharata

I recall the veteran CND campaigner, Bruce Kent, once responding to a question about religions surely causing nothing but wars. He appealed to the common Golden Rule tradition at the heart of all faiths and expressed exasperation that believers could ignore something so strong when they hated each other. Religion can be used as a force for good or evil, like many things in life.

Faith groups cooperate on social programmes in various parts of the world, bringing humanitarian aid and better health, or establishing education and housing programmes. Such forums can add an extra spiritual dimension to those of justice and peace offered by purely secular groups. As one faith leader put this:

'A person may be employed, well-fed, have adequate housing and a stable family, whilst still not being happy. We take a holistic approach.'

REVELATION AND TRUTH CLAIMS

It is one thing to see connections and overlaps in areas of human concern and general spiritual values. All of this can be traced to being made in a certain way so that the human heart is receptive to God. When we move further into the arena of special revelation it becomes much more difficult. The fact is that each religion has its own teachings and doctrines as well as aspects that everyone can agree upon. There are specific truth claims that cannot be easily reconciled, if at all. If Islam teaches that Muhammad is the Last Prophet, and Christianity teaches that Jesus is risen and is Lord and Saviour of all, and some Hindus believe that Krishna is the supreme Godhead, then we are in open contest and conflict. If you believe one of these claims, you will belong to that faith. That is not to say that you cannot see anything good in the others, or that you will be hateful and intolerant, but you cannot be where they are. You will be under a specific authority, the authority of that tradition and 'revelation'. The same point holds true for beliefs about the afterlife. You can either believe in reincarnation or in resurrection: they are totally different and incompatible.

There is a parable about five blind Hindu holy men on the banks of the Ganges:

A tame elephant wandered among them one day. One reached out and touched its body; he thought it was a wall of mud.

One touched its tusks and thought there were two spears.

One touched its trunk and thought it was a serpent.

One touched its tail and thought it was a piece of rope.

The last one laughed at them and held onto its leg. He said it was a tree, after all.

A child walked by and asked, 'Why are you all holding the elephant?'

This parable is used by Hinduism to teach that there is truth in all faiths and that each one has an angle on God but not the complete picture. Other, similar, illustrations involve the fingers of the hand. All lead to the palm at the centre, just as all rivers flow into the sea. Some faiths and some individual believers do believe this, and it is tempting to overemphasize the similarities. One model of inter-faith dialogue is to blend the faiths together into a bland 'soup'. In fact, this does them few favours. Each faith has distinctive features and beliefs and these should be able to stand by themselves. They should not be reduced and watered down. Too often members of some faiths enter forums and are surprised at how apologetic some others are about differences. Many Christians who are involved tend to ignore distinctions and awkward clashes of truth claims. Muslims, however, tend to have a strong self-identity and a robust faith. They often like people to hear who they are, and they like to hear who their colleagues are. True dialogue can only be born of honesty. As Kipling once said:

If a group of blind men found an elephant and touched different parts of it, what would each one describe?

'But there is neither East nor West, Border, nor Breed, nor Birth, When two strong men stand face to face, though they come from the ends of the earth!'

The theologian Hans Küng once remarked that there will be no world peace until there is peace between the religions. This need not mean a false peace as the faiths pretend to be something that they are not, pruning themselves of the awkward differences. It means listening to each other, agreeing to disagree, being tolerant but committed, deeply committed to your own position. We can disagree in charity.

EXAMPLES OF DIALOGUE

Listening to another tradition can be a duty of citizenship. It can lead to increased levels of cooperation in development or peace and justice issues. It can overcome prejudice and racism. It can also open our own eyes to aspects of our own tradition that we have forgotten or which have become neglected. I knew of a Christian priest who sat with Western Buddhists for a simple meditation exercise. This was not explicitly Buddhist, using Buddhist chants; it was simply a relaxation exercise in which the people imagined that they were taking one step at a time into clean, warm sand. It was to encourage people to live in the present, for the present; the 'now' has a grace about it as we step away from the past. The priest talked at depth with the leader about the Christian spirituality of the sacrament of the present moment. There was a real moment of sharing and mutual illumination. The Buddhist practice had reawakened a Christian insight.

Gandhi drew inspiration from the ethical teaching of Jesus in the Sermon on the Mount and drew this into his adoption of the Jain principle of non-violence, *ahimsá*.

Such interreligious dialogue often takes place in monastic communities. A Roman Catholic retreat once invited a Buddhist monk to speak to them. He told them to use the cross as their *koan*, a pithy and wise saying to meditate upon. *Koans* tease open perceptions and often reverse values. The cross as a symbol certainly does that. The Buddhist monk also recognized his own hope of enlightenment, of *samadhi*, and of entering the bliss of *nirvana* in the hope of resurrection. The doctrines and terms were very different, but there was a resonance, a common spiritual hope.

Thomas Merton, the celebrated Trappist monk, journeyed east towards the end of his life and conversed with the Dalai Lama and others. He concluded that his time with the Dalai Lama had been warm and instructive:

'It was a very warm and cordial discussion, and at the end I felt we had become very good friends and were somehow quite close to each other. I felt a great respect and fondness for him as a person... He remarked that I was a "Catholic gesh"...'

This title was the highest honour that someone like the Dalai Lama could bestow, and it was like an honorary doctorate.

The recently discovered cache of Jesus Sutras in China dating from the first millennium reveals a sensitive and tolerant dialogue between Christian monks and Taoists and Buddhists. Eastern terms were used to elucidate Christian belief, such as calling the saints 'Dharma Lords', that is, ones who had mastered the Way of Truth. There were bold and loving portrayals of the hope in Christ that could set people free from the curse of bad *karma*, expressed in the language and thought forms of the local people.

Such open-hearted learning and sharing is possible, even with huge differences.

We must also recognize the difficult, the dark and the frankly demonic in each other's traditions. There might be doctrines and practices that are very unattractive and disturbing. This can be the case within the Christian tradition too, such as the vile hatred between Catholic and Protestant during the Reformation, or the bloodlust of some of the Crusaders. Humility points the finger at oneself first.

THE PATTERN

Ninian Smart eventually identified seven dimensions of religion:
- ❧ the ritual dimension
- ❧ the experiential dimension
- ❧ the mythic dimension
- ❧ the doctrinal dimension
- ❧ the ethical dimension
- ❧ the social dimension
- ❧ the artistic dimension

There are other ways of carving up religions into slices for analysis, but this model has been influential. It is good to see the experiential dimension near the top of the list, for the reasons we mentioned earlier. However, it is perhaps still too much like an exercise in dissection or arranging the pieces under a microscope. A religion is a living whole in which all these dimensions come into play. As I am taking a more spiritual approach, emphasizing religions as Ways that people follow, I have selected several categories for looking at each faith from this more personal angle. What does it mean for someone to belong to such a faith? There will be important beliefs that are very precious to the believer, for example, rather than abstract lists and accounts that are cut adrift from their original contexts. The pattern of each faith chapter is as follows:

1. An introduction, giving an overview of the faith and summing up its special character, insight or focus – its 'genius'.
2. First Steps, tracing the founders and beginnings.
3. The Goal, looking at the most important beliefs and the focus of worship.
4. Teachers of the Way, looking at Scriptures and the guidance they bring.
5. Treasury of the Heart, looking at beliefs that are held as great treasures by adherents.
6. Paths to Peace, looking at ways of praying and meditating, as well as key values.
7. Awe and Wonder, examining the place of worship and ritual.
8. Journey into Mystery, exploring rites of passage, key symbols and the way that mystery is affirmed and handled.
9. Making Merry, looking at festivals and pilgrimage.
10. Today, examining key issues for the believers in today's society.

The experience of awe at the vastness and beauty of nature can be seen as a spiritual feeling.

A SPIRITUALITY EXERCISE

To enter into the spirit of our selection and the pattern of the chapters, the following exercise takes each category and applies it to an individual. Take some time to explore this.

1. Thinking of the 'genius', reflect upon special things about yourself. What do people appreciate about you? What skills do you have?

2. First Steps can be an opportunity to reflect upon your life up until now. Trace a lifeline, marking on key dates and experiences, good and bad, secular and sacred.

3. The Goal asks you to think about the really important aims in your life, or the important people. Besides making a list of these, you could also assemble a collection of magazines and search through them for any pictures that inspire you. Collect these and make them into as a collage. See what emerges and what it says about you.

4. Teachers of the Way asks you to assemble a scrapbook of key and influential people and books that have had an impact on you and guided your life.

5. Treasury of the Heart gets you to think about the treasure in your life, be it inner qualities, beliefs, skills, objects or people.

6. Paths to Peace seeks to get you to explore how you find peace in your life. Have you a method or a place of prayer? What do you do to relax?

7. Awe and Wonder asks you to explore your experiences of awe in life and in nature such as the birth of a child or standing on a hill watching a sunrise.

8. Journey into Mystery asks you to collect important symbols of things in your life, or to make up your own symbols. Think, too, of times when you have been aware of mystery, such as a time of suffering when there seemed to be no answers, or when you looked at the night sky and wondered about the vastness and what it all means.

9. Making Merry asks you to recall times of great celebration.

10. Today brings you into the present and asks you to reflect upon why you want to read about various world faiths. What are you searching for?

At this point, I will hand over to you to begin the search and the exploration. I rejoice in anything that is good and true in any faith, even though I affirm fidelity to Jesus, as he is described in one Anglican prayer:

> '*You raised up Jesus to be our Saviour,*
> *born of Mary,*
> *to be the living bread,*
> *in whom all our hungers*
> *are satisfied.*'

I hope that I have been as fair as possible to each faith within the light and honesty of my own faith. I have sought to be fair and balanced, even when describing rituals and beliefs that could never be my own. But then again, I am only human, and such neutrality is ultimately impossible. You can never sever the observer from the object under scrutiny. Perhaps, at best, I am training as a juggler.

Kevin O'Donnell

Hinduism

'O God, lead us from untruth to truth. Lead us from darkness to light and lead us from death to immortality.'

The *Upanishads*

THE ANCIENT FAITH?

There are about 900 million Hindus in the world today, in many countries. The majority live in India. Hindus believe that their faith is the oldest known to humanity. The term 'Hinduism' is relatively late, pertaining to the creeds of those in the Indus Valley. Hindus call their faith *Sanatana dharma*, the Eternal Law or Way. Versions of what we now call Hinduism can be traced back to about 3000 BCE at least. What exact shape it had prior to this no one knows as so much about the past is lost to us without artefacts or written records. The faith also grew and developed over the centuries from a basic, common matrix of concepts. There were key eras of development, particularly the sixth century BCE.

AN EXOTIC PLANT?

Hinduism includes many different approaches, spiritualities and beliefs about God and the gods, and some of its rituals go back millennia. Hinduism is often compared to an exotic growth of many layers and branches, with ancient, even quite primitive aspects surviving alongside more sublime and philosophical ideas. It is as though the ancient Greek religion with Zeus and the pantheon of gods survived intact after Hellenistic society adopted monotheism and philosophy, even absorbing Christianity into its spiritual soup. This did not happen, of course, and instead earlier ideas were rejected in favour of newer ones. Not so in Hinduism.

ONE OR MANY?

Hindus have different ideas about God. There are, at least on the surface, many gods. Homes and temples contain various images of deities. There are four schools of thought about the gods:

1. There are many gods, and some Hindus practise a form of polytheism.

2. There is only one God, and all the deities are aspects of God, symbols of him. Thus, power, light, creativity, judgement and so forth are all pictured as separate beings.

3. There is one God but many exalted, divine beings who are like the angels and saints in Christianity. Only God took human form in the series of *avatars* such as Vishnu or Krishna, but other deities are either superior beings or exalted souls of purified human beings.

4. Some see God (and therefore all the deities too) as an impersonal life force, an energy. Others stress that God is personal and can be related to.

COMING TO THE WEST

Hinduism has travelled with patterns of immigration, especially to parts of the former British empire. The late twentieth century saw an increased interest in Hindu teaching and devotion in the West. Pop stars met with Indian gurus or have embraced aspects of the faith and musical style, and the International Society for Krishna Consciousness (ISKON) was started in the 1960s by a Hindu holy man, Bhaktivedanta Swami Prabhupada.

In a nutshell

Hinduism is a very old religious system rooted in India. Lofty ideas about monotheism exist alongside village shrines to ancestral deities or spirits. A series of rituals and devotions help the person make a long journey back to the Source of life, back to God. This journey can last many lifetimes, and Hindus teach reincarnation. Each individual is believed to have a spark of the divine, the *atman* or soul, within them. This is destined to return to God. Worship can be exotic and colourful, lively and joyful, with many symbols and offerings.

The genius

Hinduism practises a wide-ranging tolerance for other paths and faiths, recognizing many routes that lead to God. It manages to allow very different ideas and beliefs to coexist and to allow

The Beatles surround the Hindu Guru Maharishi.

various spiritual paths to be followed within the one faith.

The symbol

The *Aum* or Om syllable is written in ancient Sanskrit. This is chanted and is believed by many to represent the basic vibrations of energy by which the universe was created.

First Steps

'Whilst everything around me is ever changing, ever dying, there is underlying all that changes a living power that is changeless, that holds all together, that creates, dissolves and recreates. That power or spirit is God.'

Mohandas Gandhi

ANCIENT REMAINS

Archeologists have excavated the remains of an ancient city in the Indus Valley, Mohenjo-daro. This dates from around 3000 BCE and was one of a cluster of large cities built in the Indus Valley.

The ruins of the ancient city of Mohenjo-daro in India.

There were paved streets and brick houses with a drainage system. This was far in advance of the dwellings of many other ancient peoples of the time. We cannot tell what their religion was like in any detail, but various artefacts have been found. There are statues of goddesses that are discoloured by smoke as though lamps had been left burning in front of them. The dead seem to have been buried at that time (in later Hindu ritual they would be cremated), and bowls placed as offerings with the dead have pictures of animals and what look like gods and goddesses on them. There is also a clay seal that has a figure of a deity in the lotus position, which could be a primitive image of the Hindu god Shiva. The script on this cannot be deciphered – it is an unknown language.

There is also evidence of ritual bathing to purify oneself before worship, and of gathering around ceremonial fires. Such purification rites and offerings at a sacred fire are still practised in modern-day Hinduism.

THE ARYAN PEOPLE

The Aryan people moved to the Indus Valley from Central Asia in about 1500 BCE. They conquered the land and imposed their customs, also absorbing some of the earlier traditions and carrying them on as groups settled down peacefully with the earlier inhabitants and intermarrying. 'Aryan' means 'noble people'. There is archaeological evidence to show that animals were sacrificed on the sacred fires at this time – blood and food offerings to appease the gods and to seek blessing.

The Aryan deities seem to have been connected with the sky, the sun and the

Bhakti

Bhakti yoga means 'The Way of Devotion'. This means of finding God uses joyful praise to honour the divine. *Bhakti* devotees usually worship Shiva or Vishnu as personal forms of God. *Bhakti* flourished in the Middle Ages, when the popular stories about the god Krishna were used by the sage Caitanya (1486–1534) in Bengal to forge a new style of devotion to Krishna as the Supreme Godhead rather than Vishnu. Devotees can have distinctive markings on their foreheads. They often have a tuft of hair growing on a shaved head like a flag on a flagpole flying in honour of God. Other traditions say that Krishna will pull the devotee up to heaven by this.

wind. Indra, the thunder god, was one of their most popular deities. They believed that this warrior god had helped them conquer the land: 'who has been a match for everyone, who moves the immovable; he, O man, is Indra'. It is thought that the Aryans began what became the caste system, introducing the idea of *varnas* or castes of people. They probably reduced the Indus people to the two lower castes of *vaishyas* (merchants) and *sudras* (unskilled labourers). The Aryans were the two senior *varnas* of the *brahmins* (the priests) and the *kshatriyas* (warriors). How rigid and prescribed this was in early times is debated by scholars, however.

THE *VEDAS*

Scriptures gradually took form as the *Vedas* (meaning 'knowledge'), which contained details of sacrifices, deities and praise to God. By the sixth century BCE men were renouncing material possessions and careers to sit at the feet of teachers, gurus, in the forests. They debated metaphysics, the gods and methods of devotion. They devised a means of meditation to free the mind from earthly attachments and desires, to seek higher truth and to seek the divine. This became known as *jnana* yoga, meaning 'The Way of Meditation and Self-Control'. The idea of God as an impersonal force indwelling all things, and the *atman* as a spark of this divine light came from their teachings.

TALES OF HEROISM

Hinduism has a rich deposit of stories about heroes, gods, warriors and sages. Many of these take place in ancient times, before recorded history as we know it, and can take the form of huge sagas full of epic battles, love stories and teaching. There are also law codes such as that of Manu written in around 200 CE. There are many deities, many heroes, many teachers along the way, but no single founder for this ancient faith.

The Goal

'You are woman. You are man.
You are the dark blue bee
And the green parrot with
    the red eyes.
The lightning is your child.
You are the seasons of the year
    and the sea.
You are part of everything.
You are everywhere.
Everywhere that is, is born of you.'

The *Upanishads*

EARLY BELIEFS

The earliest *Vedic* Scriptures mention various deities, but there are frequent hymns of praise to Varuna, the god who forgives:

'I glorify Varuna almighty, the God who is loving towards him who adores. We praise thee with our thoughts, O God. We praise thee even as the sun praises thee in the morning; may we find joy in being thy servants.

Remove all fear from me, O Lord. Receive me graciously unto thee, O King… We will sing thy praises, O God almighty. We will now and evermore sing thy praises, even as they were sung of old. For thy laws are immutable, O God: they are firm like the mountains…'

Rg Veda 11.28.1–9

Another early hymn searches for the ultimate God, the High God, the One who is eternal. The hymn questions and puzzles over time, eternity and creation:

'There was not then what is nor what is not. There was no sky and no heaven beyond the sky. What power was there? Where? Who was that power? Was there an abyss of fathomless waters?

'There was neither death nor immortality then. No signs were there of night and day. The One was breathing by its own power, in deep peace. Only the One was; there was nothing beyond… And in the One arose love. Love the first seed of soul. The truth of this the sages found in their hearts…'

Rg Veda 10.129

Avatars of Vishnu

Another ancient Hindu tradition is that Vishnu – simply 'God' to many Hindus – has taken animal and human form several times in history to teach humanity. These appearances or forms are known as the *avatars*.

There are ten *avatars* described in Hindu literature; the first six are animals, or semi-human, and the last four are human. Some Hindus include fewer, omitting the Buddha, and some would add teachers such as Jesus.

1. The fish Manu who warned about the Flood.
2. A tortoise who formed the ocean to allow life to come forth.
3. A boar who fought a demon and saved the earth.
4. A man-lion who destroyed a demon who forbade people to worship God.
5. A dwarf who destroyed a demon through trickery and by growing to immense size.
6. Parasu-rama, a hero who saved many priests from being killed.
7. Rama, a prince who defeated the evil Ravana and rescued his wife, Sita.
8. Krishna the goatherd who taught Arjuna the mysteries in the *Bhagavad Gita*.
9. The Buddha who taught enlightenment.
10. Kalki, an *avatar* yet to come who will end this present age and bring peace.

Some of the demon kings mentioned are seen as human beings who gained great powers through the wrong use of meditation.

All but the last two are supposed to have lived millennia ago. Krishna, for example, is said to have lived about 5,000 years ago.

The *avatars* are real but illusions at one and the same time. The god can break free at will and cannot be overcome or suffer. This can be seen in some of the popular stories about Krishna, for example. In one his mother scolds him for stealing some butter from her. She tries to tie him up with a rope, but it will not reach around him – he is really vaster than the universe. In another story, he opens his mouth to reveal the universe spinning inside it. The *avatars* are not the same as incarnations in the Christian sense; Christians believe that God took flesh and could suffer, utterly committed to the act of incarnation. *Avatars* are more like manifestations or appearances.

BRAHMAN AND *ATMAN*

The search for the One, the Eternal and the Unknown exercised the minds and hearts of sages and gurus for many years thereafter. The sixth century BCE formulated the ideas about *Brahman*, a word linked with growth and creativity. *Brahman* is the Truth of the universe, the Whole, the Fullness of existence. The *atman* is the Truth of the heart, the inner self or the soul. The sacred syllable, *Aum*, can be applied to *Brahman* and the *atman*.

One of the *Upanishads*, the sacred texts of the forest gurus, asks a question:

> *'When a man dies, this doubt arises: some say "he is" and some say "he is not". Teach me the truth...'*

The answer comes:

> *' "The atman, the self, is never born and never dies." '*
>
> *Katha Upanishad*

THE HINDU TRINITY?

Some Hindu traditions have three deities, Brahma, Vishnu and Shiva, as three gods in a triad of power. Brahma is the creator, Vishnu the preserver and Shiva the destroyer (ending and cleansing to allow a new beginning). Other traditions have these gods individually acting as the creator. There are many stories and myths of the gods that cannot all be made into a coherent unity. Some images of Shiva show him dancing the creation of the universe, for example, with musical instruments, many arms to denote strength and a circle of fire around him to suggest eternity and power.

Teachers of the Way

'Do not do to another what you would not like to be done to yourself; that is the meaning of the law — all other laws are variable.'

Mahabharata

THE *SHASTRAS*

The Hindu term for Scriptures is *Shastras*. There are many different Scriptures that were written down over the centuries as Hinduism developed. The greatest and most revered collection is called the *Vedas*, from the word meaning 'knowledge'. The *Vedic* literature covers many hymns and also the metaphysical discourses of *gurus* and their disciples. The latter are called the *Upanishads*, meaning 'to sit at the feet of a Master'. The earliest *Vedic* texts are the *Rg Veda*, which contain many hymns to the gods, some dating back to the Aryan times about 3,000 years ago. The *Vedas* as a whole contain scientific, medical and mathematical knowledge that was advanced for its time.

The *Vedas* are not easy to understand. They are written in the ancient language of Sanskrit and have to be explained in Hindi or other local dialects by the priests. There are complicated concepts in the *Vedas*, and various commentaries have been produced by the Brahmins, known as *Smritis*.

Shiva dancing the dance of creation, surrounded by a circle of fire, and standing upon an evil demon.

The *Bhagavad Gita*

Bhagavad Gita means 'The Song of the Lord', and this is one of the most popular Scriptures for Hindus. It is part of the epic text of the *Mahabharata*, as the two armies face each other, ready to do battle. Prince Arjuna is ready in his chariot, but he is concerned and afraid because he has to fight members of his own family. His charioteer, Krishna, counsels him. Krishna teaches about duty, *dharma*, and the eternal nature of the *atman*. He leads Arjuna through the paths of the various yogas — *karma* yoga, in which good deeds purify the soul; *jnana* yoga, in which meditation brings closeness to God; and *bhakti* yoga, the way of praise and devotion to a god.

Krishna teaches Arjuna to worship him as God, and the *Gita* ends with a revelation of Krishna as a divine being.

THE EPICS

Stories entertain and teach truth easier than long discourses or hymns. Hindus have many such collections which contain enlightening parables and stories. The greatest are the *Mahabharata* and the *Ramayana*.

The *Mahabharata* is the great history of ancient India. It is an epic about a struggle between good and evil, centred around a struggle for the throne and the danger to the lives of five princes.

A blind prince was next in line to succeed, but as he was not eligible, he stepped aside to offer the crown to his brother, Pandu. Pandu renounced the throne in order to become a holy man, a *sadhu* or *sanyasi*. He handed it to his brother, Dhritarashtra. Dhritarashtra took Pandu's five sons into the palace to care for them after their father renounced everything and lived as a holy man. He treated his brother's sons as his own. The king's own sons became jealous and sought to kill their cousins. Prince Arjuna helped the sons of Pandu to escape to the forest. Pandu heard of this and granted his sons a half of his kingdom, but a great battle raged for eighteen days. Pandu's sons won and ruled wisely. The *Ramayana* relates the attempt of Prince Rama to free his wife, Sita, from the demon king Ravana.

PARABLES

Hinduism has many parables. In some of these, Krishna reveals his divine nature and spiritual wisdom. For example, the story of Krishna and the *gopi* (cowherd) girls tells how he hid the clothes of the girls when they were bathing in the river. To retrieve them, they have to come before him one by one, totally naked, and bow in worship. On the surface this story sounds scandalous, but it is given a spiritual interpretation: the soul must be honest and bare before God.

The story of the Rasa dance has the *gopi* girls singing and praising with Krishna by the river. Krishna goes ahead with his favourite, Radha. The others become jealous, and they lose sight of him. Then they find Radha in tears; she has become proud that Krishna wanted her, and now he has disappeared. Only when they change their attitudes does Krishna reappear. Pride makes God withdraw; humility welcomes him.

PEOPLE

The eighteenth to twentieth centuries have seen some committed and outstanding spokesmen for Hinduism. This was the age when the East was in contact with the Western powers through empire and trade. These various men were concerned to reform aspects of Hindu society to allow India to progress and benefit from Western contacts and the age of rationalism. They tended to move away from a more basic, primitive belief in deities and gravitated towards the idea of a pure monotheism, a belief in the oneness of God which underpinned Islam and Christianity also. They wanted tolerance and respect between faiths.

Ram Mohan Roy (1772–1833) worked in Bengal where the East India Company was based. He had been educated in a Muslim centre on the Ganges, and then he studied Sanskrit. He translated some of the *Upanishads* into English, trying to show that Hinduism was based upon the oneness of God. He also wrote about the teaching of Jesus, seeing this as vibrant and ethical, but he rejected other Christian doctrines as later, mythical

Krishna and Prince Arjuna riding their chariot into battle.

overlays. His stripped-down Christ fitted smoothly into his worldview. Debendranath Tagore (1817–1905) worked with Roy's 'Divine Society' for social reform in Hinduism, relaxing the caste system and being open to the Untouchables, the lowest rank of society in classical India. Ramakrishna (1834–86) began as an ardent devotee of Kali, the Mother goddess, following the path of *bhakti* but experiencing excessive ecstasies. He developed forms of *jnana* yoga, meditating and claiming to reach the highest mental state whereby God, the soul and all deities merge as one reality. He also turned to the teachings of other faiths, meditating upon Allah and Christ. His experiences convinced him that all faiths were in harmony.

Treasury of the Heart

> '*A wife loves her husband not for his own sake… but because the* atman *lives in him… children are loved not for their own sake, but because the* atman *lives in them.*'
>
> The *Upanishads*

TAT TVAM ASI

The *Upanishads* sum up the teaching about divinity and the human being as *tat tvam asi*, 'That You Are!' A story explains this.

A spiritual master was asked by his disciple where God was. He took a bowl of water and told the disciple to put salt into it. He did so. Then the master asked the boy to drink from one side. 'Can you taste the salt?' he asked. 'Yes.'

Then the bowl was turned round and the question asked again and again until the boy drank from every side. The salt was all through the water, everywhere. *Brahman* was a force all through the universe. But the master added, 'That you are!' teaching that our true self is part of God. This is the root idea of many New Age teachings today that the inner self is divine; the New Age movement draws much inspiration from Eastern religions.

The *atman* is to be understood as an eternal reality, a part of *Brahman* within each person. This is not the same as the Christian idea of the immortal soul, which is held to be a gift of the Creator.

Hindus bow, clasping their hands in a position of worship when they meet each other. They say *Namaste*, which means 'I bow to you in respect.' This is to honour the *atman* within the other person.

Parables are told to explain about the *atman*. Two birds dwelt in a tree. The smaller one enjoyed the fruit and felt the protection of the larger bird above as it spread out its wings. The tree is the body; the smaller bird is the *atman* and the larger is *Brahman*. Or again, the sunlight streams into a room, but a light bulb within it also sheds light. The greater light is God, the lesser is the *atman*.

DHARMA

Dharma can be translated as 'duty' or as 'Way' or 'Teaching'. It is something to be obeyed and followed. 'Duty' means to act righteously. This can mean standing up for what is right and fighting against injustice. This can involve non-violent protest, *ahimsa*, as practised by Gandhi, or it is permissible to fight in a war in a just cause, as Krishna taught Prince Arjuna in the *Bhagavad Gita*.

'If the light of a thousand suns suddenly arose in the sky, that splendour might be compared to the radiance of the Supreme Spirit.'
Krishna,
Bhagavad Gita 11:12

'I see the splendour of an infinite beauty which illumines the whole universe. It is thee! With thy crown and sceptre and circle. How difficult thou art to see! But I see thee: as fire, as the sun, blinding, incomprehensible.'
Arjuna to Krishna,
Bhagavad Gita 11:16

'Though all ancient texts are sacred, all are open to figurative interpretation; unlike Islam and… Protestant Christianity, Hinduism has never depended on the letter of the Scriptures. Thus there is every possibility of its adapting itself to… rapidly changing conditions'
A.L. Basham, 'Hinduism', in
The Concise Encyclopedia of Living Faiths

❊

'When I need to relax, I go to feed and care for the cows. That is an honour and a joy that brings great peace.'
ISKON devotee at Bhaktivedanta Manor

'Peacefulness, self-control, austerity, purity, tolerance, honesty, knowledge, wisdom and religiousness – they are the qualities by which the Brahmins work righteousness.'
Bhagavad Gita 18:42

'When they divided Primal Man, how many divisions did they make? What was his mouth? What his arms? The *Brahmin* was his mouth. The *Kshatriya* [warrior] his arms. His thighs the *Vaisya* [merchant]. The *Sudra* [labourers] his feet.'
Rg Veda 10

Karma

Hindus believe in *karma*. This word is often translated 'fate', but although *karma* is an impersonal force or principle, it is not blind fate. *Karma* is rather the power of your actions over a lifetime or several lifetimes. This is rather like the ripples that spread out in a pool after throwing in a rock. Actions have consequences that live after them, rather like the Christian teaching that we sow what we reap. *Karma* is thus an accumulation, an energy that decides your fate.

Unlike Christianity, Hinduism believes in many reincarnations and the cycle of rebirth, *samsara*. Each rebirth is believed to come as a result of previous deeds and your accumulated *karma*. Life is illusion, *maya*, a lesser reality than that of the eternal reality of *Brahman* or the divine. Hindus seek to be released from the cycle of *samsara* into union with the divine, into perfect bliss. This release is known as *moksha*, liberation. They believe that it might take many lifetimes to become pure enough and free of bad *karma*.

For some Hindu traditions, this release and union is impersonal, like a raindrop falling back into the ocean. In other traditions, such as the Vishnaic, or the *bhakti* movement, it is personal. The raindrop retains consciousness and enjoys bliss in the presence of the Lord. *Bhakti* movements also tend to have an idea of a personal heaven, enjoying the presence of God.

Dharma also involves respect for nature and the environment, honouring the presence of God in all living things and the *atman* within animals and humans. The earth is seen as Mother as we all depend upon nature for our livelihood. We are to respect nature in return. All motherhood is seen as sacred within Hinduism, whether in nature or through childbirth, whether that of a cow or that of a goddess.

Forests and gardens are seen as sacred groves, places of divine presence and beauty.

Hindus are encouraged to be vegetarian, though this is expected only of priests, wandering holy men, *sadhus*, and certain devotees such as the members of ISKON.

SACRED COWS
The cow has been seen as sacred in Hinduism for centuries. This probably dates from the Aryan invasion when they were used widely for their milk and their hides when they died. In rural Indian life they are immensely beneficial creatures for humans. They provide milk which makes butter, *ghee*, yoghurt, cream and cheese. *Ghee* is used in offerings. The cows also pull carts and ploughs on the land, milling corn and ploughing irrigation channels. Dried cow dung is used on walls and as fuel for fires. Cows are purposeful, utility animals seen as 'mothers' or gifts of the gods. They are not to be killed and beef is forbidden meat. Hindu centres – *ashrams* where people live in community and worship – often have cow sanctuaries, and looking after them and using them on the land is a central part of the daily round and godly devotion.

Caste and *Dharma*

One's caste, *varna*, is determined by *karma*. The Laws of Manu (c. 200 CE) defined the roles of each caste and their duties. This became a rigid system determining employment and marriage rights. It is seen as one's *dharma* to fulfil these laws. However, there is another, more liberating tradition in Hinduism. Here, a person's inner nature and character can determine their status and rights. This is a more spiritual understanding of caste. This seems to be taught in the *Bhagavad Gita*.

There are cases of Brahmin gurus accepting lower caste members as devotees after they have shown that they have the necessary understanding, desire and truth of character. As one said to a young man who had been born illegitimately, unsure who his father was, 'I accept you as a Brahmin, for your soul is honest.'

It is on this basis that ISKON members can be accepted as Brahmin priests in parts of India though they are Westerners by birth.

Paths to Peace

> '*I believe that if Untouchability is really rooted out, it will purge Hinduism of a terrible blot. My fight against untouchability is a fight against the impure in humanity… My cry will rise to the throne of the Almighty God.*'
>
> Mohandas Gandhi

YOGA

Yoga is 'the way of union'. The word also suggests a yoke that binds oxen together and guides their steps. Hinduism has several forms of yoga, only one of which involves physical exercises. The form of yoga practised for health in the West is *hatha* yoga, the first stage of a series of exercises and disciplines to help a person to meditate. This is *jnana* yoga, a way to focus, to purify the mind and to practise non-attachment to material things. One mental exercise for the initiated is to imagine the faces of loved ones and then of enemies and to cultivate an attitude of indifference and detachment.

Two other forms of yoga involve works and praise. *Karma* yoga seeks to attain good, positive *karma* by charitable actions. *Bhakti* yoga is about devotion to a personal deity.

CHANTS

Hindus have *mantras* that they can use for meditation or for *bhakti* praise. A *guru* might give a disciple a particular *mantra*, which will usually invoke the names of Hindu gods. *Mantras* are short sentences that are repeated over and over again, slowly, letting the rhythms and the meaning sink deep into the mind. ISKON uses the 'Hare Krishna' mantra.

A member of the International Society for Krishna Consciousness looks after a calf on their farm in England.

Mohandas Gandhi and non-violence

Ahimsa means 'non-violence' or the avoidance of injury to any sentient being. It is mentioned in the *Upanishads* but gained prominence in Hinduism in modern times following its espousal by Mohandas K. Gandhi (1869–1948). His regard for this principle may stem from his Jain friends. (In fact, *ahimsa* derives from Buddhism: it is the first of the Five Precepts of Buddhist life. For Jains, it is equally important as it is the first of the Five Great Vows. For Jains, *ahimsa* means not taking or hurting any life, and Jain holy men wear white cloths over their mouths so that they do not, inadvertently, swallow any insects. They will also sweep the floor in front of them so that they do not step on any living thing.)

Mohandas K. Gandhi was born in a Jain district of India. He was influenced by the Jain holy men of his childhood, particularly one Raichand Bhai whom he writes about in his autobiography.

Gandhi travelled to England to study law in 1888. He began to study Hinduism more deeply as a result of living in a foreign culture where many questioned him. It was at this time that he became devoted to the *Bhagavad Gita*.

Gandhi led protests in South Africa against the laws that all Indians had to carry an identity card and thus were seen as second-class citizens. He started to follow *ahimsa*, non-violent protest. He carried this on back in India when he returned in 1915. He formed a religious community, an *ashram*. This was to be open to anyone, and he took a family of *Dalits*, Untouchables, into the *ashram*. He called them *Harijans*, 'Children of God'. He began a well-publicised fast on behalf of the *Harijans*, and many temples began to open their doors to them as a result. Another example of a non-violent protest was the salt march of 1930. The British government had put a tax on salt, and so he led the people to the sea and taught them how to boil sea water to make their own salt.

Gandhi said that *ahimsa* was the 'force of truth', *satyagraha*. It spoke volumes, challenged, pricked the conscience and shamed the powerful and corrupt.

Gandhi was assassinated in 1948 by a Hindu extremist after leading the nation to independence from Britain in 1947.

'Hare Krishna, Hare Krishna,
Krishna, Krishna, Hare, Hare,
Hare Rama, Hare Rama,
Rama, Rama, Hare, Hare.'

Rama was another name for God, an appearance or *avatar* of Vishnu. Hare was another name for Krishna's consort, Radha.

REVERENCE FOR LIFE

Hinduism teaches a reverence for life. If God indwells all living things, then respecting them is a form of worship. Many Hindus endeavour to live a vegetarian lifestyle, though this is not binding on any except the priests. This is to practise *ahimsa* and to respect that animals carry the *atman* within. They believe that a person might be reborn as an animal. ISKON have stricter discipline for all their devotees. They are expected to live on a diet that is basically milk, nuts, yoghurt and fruit. They are taught that a meat eater will be reborn as an animal or will have a violent death.

Reverence for nature naturally flows from the sense of God in living things. There is a saying in the *Mahabharata* that states, 'even if there is only one tree full of flowers and fruits in a village, that place becomes worthy of worship and respect'.

MOTHER GANGA

The River Ganges is a sacred river to Hindus, being called 'Mother Ganga'. On the one hand, it is a river that flows down from the snow-covered mountains of the Himalayas. On the other hand, it is spiritual, coming down as a gift from Shiva. Hindus seek to bathe in its waters, believing that this will cleanse them of sins. The holy city of Varanasi, or Benares, stands on the banks of the Ganges. Thousands gather there, rising very early and bathing in the waters. Many have their bodies cremated there and their ashes scattered on the water.

Awe and Wonder

'If one offers Me with love and devotion a leaf, a flower, a fruit or water I will accept it.'

Krishna, *Bhagavad Gita*

ISHTA DEVATA

Hindus have a concept of 'the chosen deity', *ishta devata*. This means that God can be worshipped through one image, one of the gods. A person might become a devotee of Shiva, Vishnu, Krishna or Kali, for example. There is a famous

Gandhi on the steps of 10 Downing Street, London, on his visit to Britain in 1931.

*Hindu pilgrims bathe in
the River Ganges.*

story of a child asking a grandmother
about the number of gods:

*'How many gods are there?'
'Three thousand gods.'
The child asked again, 'How many
gods are there?'
'Three hundred.'
Again the child asked, 'How many
gods are there?'
'Three.'
One last time, the child quizzed the
grandmother, 'How many gods are
there?'
'One only!'*

Though some Hindus are polytheists, in
practice, many worship God in one
form. They will often wear markings in

clay on their foreheads and other parts
of their bodies that are symbols of their
chosen deity. Krishna devotees can mark
many points of their bodies with clay –
the forehead, the belly, the chest, the
throat, between the collar bones, both
arms, both sides of the waist, the upper
and lower back and the top of the head.
They recite thirteen names of Krishna
while doing this. This special marking
to show your *ishta devata* is known as
tilaka.

IMAGES

Images of the gods, *arca*, are set up in
shrines. These are brought in and
blessed so that the god dwells within the
image, or part of the god's presence is
encountered there. They are not just

visual aids but something akin to sacraments in the Christian tradition. Physical objects can convey the presence of the divine. The images are washed each morning, dressed in fine clothes or decorated, and food offerings are made to them. Worshippers take off their shoes to enter the temple, and some also wash their hands. They ring a bell to warn the deity that they have arrived. Going to the temple is mainly an act of devotion to visit the god. This is *darshana*, visiting the god so that the deity sees them and they see it.

Some representations of the gods can be dark and frightening; they speak of the dark side of life and the power of death as well as rebirth. Kali the Mother is often depicted as a fearsome warrior woman wearing a necklace of severed heads, a belt of severed hands and a snake around her neck. Her devotees know that she can demand sacrifice.

MANDIRS

Mandirs, or temples, are shaped like mountains, reaching up to heaven. Carvings on the exterior often show an ascent from the animals, to humans, to the gods. Inside the most sacred chamber, the inner shrine, is the image of the god. This chamber can also be called 'the womb'. Above this is a spire representing the ascent of the soul to God, in the liberation of *moksha*. The main prayer hall is supported by pillars; this is the *mandap*.

The goddess Kali after slaying an enemy.

ARTI

Each day a priest will perform during puja the *arti* ceremony. This begins and ends as the priest blows a conch shell. Then he rings the temple bell. Offerings of incense, fire and water are made to the deity. Finally, he will take a tray of lights or a lamp and move this in circular patterns around the image. Then he will pass this around the worshippers. They welcome the light, beckoning this over their faces with their hands. Chanting and lively music with drums and cymbals might also be used.

Journey into Mystery

'As a man lays aside his worn-out
clothes
And puts on others that are new,
So the soul within the body lays
aside that body
And puts on another body that
is new.
May your eyes return to the sun,
and your breath to the wind, your
waters to the ocean and your ashes
to the earth from whence they came.'

Final prayer at the Hindu
funeral ceremony

SACRED SYMBOLS

Hinduism can use:
✳ the lotus flower as a symbol of purity
✳ fire as the divine light
✳ the colour blue for the sky and thus divinity
✳ the four-sided shape that suggests good fortune from the four corners of the earth (abused by the Nazis in the Second World War)
✳ the *Aum* syllable, the sound and energy that is said to have created the universe.

PARADOX AND NON-ATTACHMENT

God, eternity, is to be found beyond the limitations of the human mind and conceptual thought. Hindu sages have often used a form of the Negative Way, the *Via Negativa*, to expound the mystery of God: 'God is not this and not that...' The eternal is not dependent upon the material world, which is an illusion of passing shapes and forms, *maya*. In this world, everything changes all the time, things are born and they die. Nothing

Puja

Puja is devotion to a deity performed in the *mandir* and at home. When performed at home, the mother of the house will ring a bell to awaken the deity and then she will wash and prepare the image or images of the family's *ishta devata*. Offerings of flowers and incense are brought, and then a little food. The impulse to honour the deity with a food offering is very strong among Hindus, and they will even try to do this when there is very little food. Such food is holy food, *prashad*.

Prayers will be offered, firstly of thanksgiving and praise, and then of supplication for various needs. These will be recited from the Hindu texts, and the *Gayatri mantra* is recited at morning *puja*:

'Peace be in the heavens; peace be on earth. May the waters flow peacefully, may the herbs and shrubs grow peacefully. May all the divine powers bring us peace. And may that peace come to us. Aum. Peace. Peace. Peace.'

Evening *puja* will involve putting the god to rest for the night.

lasts forever except the spark of the divine within each living thing, the *atman*, which needs to be set free to rejoin the ocean of the Godhead.

Yogic exercises, meditations and ascetical practices are used to free the *atman* from its attachment to earthly things and the cycle of rebirth, *samsara*.

Moksha can be seen as impersonal, rejoining the ocean, or as personal with a form of heaven. Krishna devotees, for example, speak of Krishna's abode, *Krishnaloka*, and a 'supreme planet in the spiritual sky'.

SACRED CEREMONIES

Life is charted in rituals known as *samskaras*. There are fourteen altogether. The *samskaras* of childhood number ten, including naming, taking out and presenting to the sun for the first time, the first haircut and, finally, the sacred thread ceremony.

The sacred thread is worn by young boys between the ages of 8 and 11 in the three highest castes or *varnas*. It is made of three strands of cotton, white, red and yellow. These three strands are symbolic of duties:

✻ duty to God for giving the gift of life
✻ duty to parents for giving birth to him
✻ duty to his guru or teachers for all that he has been taught.

Some see the divine triad of Brahma, Vishnu and Shiva too. Or they see symbols of the need to control their thoughts, words and actions.

The thread is worn over the left shoulder and it passes under the right arm. It is placed there, at the boy's home, by the priest. This ceremony is not compulsory, but taking the thread emphasizes certain duties and vegetarianism will be expected.

LATER *SAMSKARAS*

Other stages of life for a Hindu include marriage, raising a family, working and retirement. Retirement is an opportunity for the family to honour the parents, and they will often live with their sons and spend time in recreation and religious study and pilgrimage. This ends the

Hindu holy men on pilgrimage.

'Taking the thread was a great honour. It is like a second birth for us, and an entry into the duties of manhood.'

Ranjiv, a Hindu youth from the Caribbean

'A *sanyasi* will not have to worry about being reborn again. He is free from care and can think of God day and night. Some who sing and chant to God daily meet with God and some cross over, being taken to be with him when they are ready and they are called.'

A sanyasi in India

Early renunciation?

Some younger men choose to become *sanyasi* and never marry or follow the duties, *dharma*, laid down for other men. Theirs is a lifelong search for *moksha*. Rarely, a married man might practise renunciation and abandon a wife and children. The story of the Buddha is one such example, and another, more recent case is that of A.C. Bhaktivedanta Swami Prabhupada. Prahupada founded ISKON in 1965 in New York. He was born in Calcutta in 1896. He was a student of English, Economics and Philosophy and then became a devotee of a Hindu guru, Swami Siddharta Goswami in 1933. He wrote a masterful commentary on the *Bhagavad Gita* and worked in the pharmaceutical industry until 1950. Then he renounced his former life, leaving a wife and five children. He called this 'retiring from family life'. Under Goswami's influence, he devoted himself to Krishna as the Supreme Godhead and taught the path of Krishna Consciousness. Goswami told him to spread the teachings in the West, and ever obedient, he journeyed to New York, where, almost penniless, he worked among the youth, many of whom were affected by drugs, and began a shrine in a disused New York store. Other centres followed across the USA and Europe, and wealthy benefactors such as George Harrison of the Beatles helped their cause.

Prabhupada taught that being attached to wife and children was like a 'skin disease'; in other words, it was an attachment of the flesh and a sickness of the soul. ISKON members can marry and have children, but there are strict rules about sexual activity. It is only for procreation and the men can separate themselves as Prabhupada did.

samskaras, but there is a radical, final step that can be taken if people dare, a radical preparation for death that only a few choose to undergo.

SANYASI

To become a *sanyasi* means renouncing family, friends and all possessions. The word means 'one who has given up everything'. He wanders around the countryside with a bowl to beg for food and a water pot. His family can hold a funeral for him as though he is dead – for he has died to all earthly attachments. This radical act is to purify the soul, to cleanse bad karma and to seek *moksha* after death.

The way to God in Hinduism, ultimately, is through renunciation of the world.

Making Merry

'Life turns like the wheel, seasons come and go. Each turn helps us to remember God, our faith, and take a step further towards the light.'

Hindu Brahmin from Delhi, India

THE LUNAR CALENDAR

Hindus follow a lunar calendar for their festivals, as many ancient people did. This means that the dates of major festivals may differ from year to year in the western, solar calendar. There are numerous festivals, possibly more than in any other faith. These are either about family life, stories of the gods or the seasons. Some parts of India might celebrate the festivals for one day or several days, and customs and stories of the gods will vary.

Rice powder patterns made on the street to celebrate the New Year.

FAMILY

There are two festivals to celebrate brothers and sisters. *Bhratri Dwitiya* means 'Brothers' Day'. Brothers and sisters give presents to each other, and sisters rub sandalwood powder onto their brothers' foreheads. This is accompanied by a chanted prayer: 'With this I pray may God save you from any disease and accidental death. May your life be full of golden future.'

Raksha Bandhan is when sisters make a string bracelet with a flower intertwined for their brothers. They put this on their wrist for a week and they also receive sweets. The sisters are given some money. The string recalls a story of the god Indra when he was forced out of his kingdom by an evil king, Bali, and Vishnu gave Indra's wife a thread, which she tied onto his wrist and used to pull her husband back to safety. This also strengthened him and he defeated Bali.

Prince Rama fights the demon king, Ravanna.

NEW YEAR

The time of the New Year festival might vary, but it is usually in March or April. Many Hindu families make a banner with symbols tied to it to welcome the new year.

A piece of new cloth is tied to a bamboo pole with a cooking pot, some sugar and a leafy branch. This is fixed to the doorpost and decorated with fresh flowers. The symbols suggest the blessings that God will give them in the new year to come. This is also a time to make *Rangoli* patterns with coloured powder and rice in front of their houses. These use Hindu symbols for welcome and blessing.

DIVALI

Divali is a festival of light. It is held on the darkest nights of late autumn. A cluster of different customs and stories abound in different places at *Divali*, but the theme of light is constant. Lights or lamps, *divas*, are lit to decorate window ledges and for placing outside the door. They speak of blessing and welcome, or truth and peace conquering the darkness. Some tell the story of Prince Rama being welcomed home after defeating the evil demon Ravanna. Some invoke the goddess Lakshmi, a goddess of fortune and prosperity. She is the wife of Vishnu.

DUSSHERA

This day remembers a battle of good over evil. The story is acted out in various ways around the villages of India, often with a huge effigy of the evil Ravanna being filled with fireworks and set alight. The story of Rama and Ravanna involves the hero's search for his wife, Sita. She had been kidnapped by the demon-king of Sri Lanka, Ravanna. Rama finds the king of the birds, dying from his battle with Ravanna. He tells Rama that Sita has been taken south. The king of the monkeys sends the monkey god Hanuman to search for her and he finds her. He leads Rama to Ravanna's city on the island of Sri Lanka where he fights Ravanna, killing the many-headed monster with his arrows. As he dies, Shiva appears and asks Rama to request a blessing for killing his old enemy. Rama requests that everyone who died fighting Ravanna to help him will be restored to life. Rama and Sita then return home to great rejoicing.

Today

'Where women are respected, there lives God.'

The Laws of Manu

INDIA

Despite the tolerant nature of Hinduism, there have been tensions between faith groups in India for many years. Independence from British rule in 1947 brought a separation of India into Pakistan and India. Pakistan was to be a Muslim homeland. There are rivalries and border skirmishes to this day. Some Hindu extremists have attacked mosques, and Muslim extremists have destroyed temples, even an ancient one dedicated to Shiva. Hindu extremism is also fuelled by the westernization and secularism prevalent in parts of Indian society.

LOSING TRADITIONS

Westernization is diluting the traditions that have been passed down for generations. This is happening in prosperous, cosmopolitan areas of India that respond to business and new technologies. It is also prevalent in Hindu communities that have settled in the West. Many Hindus born in Britain, for example, have never been to India. Hindus have settled in Britain in significant numbers since the 1950s, being invited from the Commonwealth nations to help rebuild Britain after the Second World War. The grandchildren of those first settlers are now adults and somewhat distant from their roots. Pressure comes within youth culture when girls want to abandon traditional costume or boys and girls want to mix freely socially. Hindu custom has arranged marriages too, and some young people wish to avoid this, while some girls can feel pressurised.

Holi

Holi is a spring festival named after the evil princess Holika who planned to murder her nephew in a fire. She was the sister of the king of the demons. His son, Prahlad, refused to worship him and would only pray to God. Prahlad had Holika sit him on her lap beside a huge bonfire. Holika was normally immune to fire but only when she was alone. If she tried to place anyone else in the flames she would die. She forgot about this, however. Prahlad escaped and defeated his father.

Holi celebrations revolve around a huge bonfire, which children will dance around and some might try to jump over. Coconuts are offered to the flames as symbols of life.

Such festivals can also attract other stories about the gods. *Holi* involves a tale of Krishna in his boyhood when he played tricks on other boys and girls in the village. He started throwing coloured dye around. On the day after the bonfire, Hindus will pelt anyone they can find with coloured dyes. All get involved, rich and poor, old and young. It is a great leveller, when employees can attack their bosses and children can throw things at their teachers. Madhur Jaffrey tells how they prepared special concoctions as children in India: 'We combined grease with mud, slime and purple dye. The concoction was reserved for our enemies. For our best friends, we prepared a golden paint, carefully mixing real gilt and oil in a small jar.'

The positive side of this integration is a blending of styles and culture in the arts and music. Asian DJs are popular and successful, blending Indian styles with Western music. Indian music has influenced popular Western musicians for many years, from the Beatles to the more recent Kula Shaker.

CASTE

The ancient caste system is still in force but is less influential than it was. It is strongest in the villages where guilds, *jatis*, help each other and exclude certain groups. In the cities, it is illegal to discriminate against someone in employment terms because of caste. There is encouragement for the *Dalits*, formerly the Untouchables, to be educated and work their way up the social ladder. An Indian President, K.R. Narayanan, was a *Dalit*. *Dalits* can now enter temples freely, but it was not always the case. Many *Dalits* have converted to

A Hindu cremation.

Buddhism or Christianity, which ignore caste divisions and lay more merit on the individual and their state of heart.

Social prejudice still exists, though, especially among the higher castes. This affects marriage and social habits. Some will only socialize or eat with their own caste. One high-caste wife, for example, will only let her family and same-caste friends eat off plates. The servants are given clay plates that are thrown away afterwards.

WOMEN

One of the greatest challenges to traditional Hinduism and Indian society is the changing role of women. Mothers have always been revered and sisters protected, but their role has been restricted to the home. Their education until the modern era was in domestic crafts alone. Mothers are often the ones who hold *puja* in the home and teach traditions and stories to their children.

Their subservient role should not be dismissed lightly, though. They had and have great influence within the home, and the ideal of the chaste, faithful wife need not be a passive figure or a doormat. The *Mahabharata*, for example, tells the story of Draupadi who was abused and mocked by the assembled kings when her husband was away in battle. Not only did the warriors all die on the battlefield as punishment, but she felled the warrior Jayadratha with one punch! Hinduism teaches that anyone who abuses a chaste wife loses all his good *karma*.

Sati was the ancient custom of 'a devoted wife' who would throw herself on the funeral pyre of her deceased husband. The Hindu Scriptures do not promote this, and in the past it seems to have been a voluntary act. Sadly, in later years, many women were forced into this act until it was outlawed in 1829.

Widows are still expected not to remarry and to dress plainly, often having to live with their late husband's family.

Other practices come with the dowry. It has been traditional for a daughter's parents to give her gifts so that she could feel blessed and set up in her new home. This has been distorted into gifts to the husband and his family, and pressure can be applied to give beyond their means. Though this was outlawed in 1961, it is still widespread, especially in the villages. When families have daughters but no sons, they can despair and there are cases of infanticide.

India has known a female prime minister, Indira Gandhi, and there are powerful, well-educated Indian women, but the traditional mores of that culture are still in existence. Women cannot act as priests in the temples and are excluded from the sacred thread ceremony. *Bhakti* movements have encouraged them to take part as devotees, being equal with the men in their chants and praises.

> 'Hinduism is a living organism liable to growth and decay and subject to the laws of nature.'
> Mohandas Gandhi

> 'I want to be free to be a young person in Britain. I'm Asian, and I have my customs, but I also live here and not in India!'
> Hindu businesswoman in the UK

❋

HINDUISM   at a glance...

- ◆ When did it begin? – The earliest attested artefacts of Hindu worship date from c. 3500 BCE.
- ◆ The founder – There is no founder. Hinduism is very ancient, though it has developed over the centuries. Various teachers such as the forest-dwelling monks of the sixth century BCE have added to it.
- ◆ God – Many Hindus believe in one God behind the universe. Some see the many gods as aspects of the one God, naming him Brahman. Some think that only the appearances of Vishnu are aspects of God, and the others are like saints and angels. Other Hindus practise polytheism.
- ◆ Redeemer figure – There is no redeemer as such, though Hindus believe that God (Vishnu) has taken animal or human form many times to teach people.
- ◆ Scriptures – There are many Scriptures in Hinduism, from the *Vedas* to the *Upanishads* to the *Bhagavad Gita*. There are great epic stories too, such as the *Ramayana* and the *Mahabharata*, as well as law codes such as the *Laws of Manu*.
- ◆ Beliefs – God is within and behind all things. Some see him as personal, some impersonal.

The way to God is through good deeds, meditation and detachment, or devotion. There is a cycle of rebirth, *samsara*, and the soul is reincarnated many times until it is pure enough to reach God.

- ◆ Place of worship – Hindu worship is centred upon the home in a shrine. There, daily *puja* is made. *Mandirs*, or temples, house an image of a god.
- ◆ Sacred food – Hindus have vegetarianism as an ideal, though only the priests and members of certain groups such as ISKON are obligated to this. Hindus will avoid eating beef as the cow is sacred. Food offered to God in a family shrine or a *mandir* is holy, *prashad*.
- ◆ Main festivals – Hindus celebrate *Divali*, the festival of light. *Holi* has a bonfire and street games. The god Rama is remembered and there are celebrations to honour brothers and sisters.
- ◆ Key symbols – The *Aum* or Om syllable represents the energy that created the universe. The *swastika* represents good fortune and the *tilaka* clay markings on the forehead show that a person is a devotee of a particular god.

Buddhism

'Not to consider "I am this," that is freedom.'

The Buddha, the Pali Canon

RELIGION OR PHILOSOPHY?

Buddhism is something of an enigma; it is religion without God, a spiritual and ethical path. Some adherents prefer to call their way a 'philosophy of life' rather than a religion. It has beliefs, ethics and rituals, though, and deals with ultimate questions as well as everyday life spirituality.

AWAKE!

Buddhism is a way to enlightenment or awakening. This was first taught by Siddharta Gautama, the first Buddha, about 2,500 years ago. He left family and riches to seek truth and inner peace, dwelling with Hindu holy men for a time. He emerged from the spiritual ferment of that time in India with a new teaching. Something happened to him, and he stepped aside from Hindu teaching and taught a new way. The emphasis is upon the individual, the mind and the inner life, to seek calm, cleansing and virtue.

The Buddha (meaning 'Enlightened One') taught a Middle Way between asceticism and luxury, a balance and a poise for life.

NO GOD?

There is no deity in Buddhism. This can shock and confuse the interested outsider from a theistic background. It can attract and enthuse someone from an agnostic or atheistic background. Buddha placed *dharma* above the gods, the Way above theology and metaphysical speculations. It would not be fair to call him an atheist, more an agnostic. He chose to sidestep talk of deities and spoke only of the path. He affirmed spiritual reality and the need for transcendence: we are part of something much bigger, vaster and mysterious. There is an ineffable side to the cosmos.

In a nutshell

Buddhists believe in a personal path, a way to find inner peace and to escape from cravings and clinging to the material world. There is a philosophy underlying this quest, which sees the world as a place of suffering, distorted and full of illusion. The individual will go through a series of reincarnations until they attain enlightenment and can escape the cycle of rebirth.

The genius

Buddhism is a philosophy that so emphasizes the Way, that all beliefs and speculations become secondary to what can be applied to the inner life and personal development. The motto is 'What works?' rather than 'What is out there?'

The symbol

The wheel represents the teaching on the cycle of rebirth as explained above. It also speaks of emptiness, a key Buddhist idea. The wheel only works because of the hole at the centre. The spaces allow the thing to be. Buddhists empty themselves of wrong desires and false attachments to seek peace of mind and a release of creativity.

'I would like to heal the division between the sacred and the profane, between the big questions of the purpose of life and, you know, buttering your toast in the morning.'

Antony Gormley, artist, speaking of how a Buddhist vision inspires his work

✳

The Buddha meditating, seated in the lotus position.

First Steps

> *'There will come a time when the name of this hill will vanish, and these people will pass away and I will attain utter nirvana.'*

The Buddha, the Pali Canon

THE LIFE OF SIDDHARTA GAUTAMA

Siddharta Gautama (c. 563–483 BCE) was born in the foothills of the Himalayas, at Lumbini. Northern India (now the area known as Nepal) was ruled by two kings and a number of local clans. Siddharta's father, Shuddhodana, was the chieftain of the Shakya clan. The Buddha is sometimes referred to as 'Shakyamuni', the 'wise man of the Shakyas'. Siddharta lived a life of pampered luxury at the capital city of Kapilavastu. He was skilled at archery, horse-riding and swordplay, attracting the affections of a princess, Yasodhara. They were married and had a son, Rahula.

Later legends tell the story that Shuddhodana was afraid that his son might give up all that he had, and his right to inherit his father's power. This fear was rooted in the message of a local holy man, Asita, who saw Siddharta as a child. He predicted that the boy would grow up to be a great spiritual teacher and would renounce all his wealth. Siddharta was therefore protected from the outside world and its cares.

THE ASCETIC

Siddharta lived for six years with *sadhus* and went to different *gurus* to learn from them. He followed a severe form of asceticism, eating as little as possible and practising meditation and yoga for hours

Change of heart

The story goes that one day Siddharta ventured out in his chariot. In the course of that day he saw an old man walking by in the last stages of senility, then a man ravaged by a foul disease, and finally a corpse being carried to the local funeral pyre, or *ghat*, by his family. Siddharta was deeply shocked, realizing that the treasures of his palace would not protect him from any sort of decay and death in the future.

On his return journey, he saw a wandering Hindu holy man, a *sadhu*, who had renounced all his possessions. In him he sensed serenity and calmness.

After much heart-searching, Siddharta left his palace, his wife and child and journeyed into the forests to seek out a teacher, a *guru*, to guide him in the spiritual path and to help him find inner peace. He left behind all his fine clothes, taking only a simple robe. He was 29 years old.

Siddharta practised renunciation, a rare practice for the younger married man. Hinduism had, and has, a strong sense of duty and the value of family life. Renunciation is usually for those who are single or much older.

on end. He became emaciated, growing so thin that you could see his backbone through his stomach. Finally, he settled with a group of five fellow ascetics by the River Nairanjana.

Siddharta felt that he could not go on. He was nearly dying and felt no closer to his goal. He went down to the river and bathed and then accepted some milk from Nandabala, a milkmaid. His companions thought that he was returning to a life of luxury and so they abandoned him.

AWAKENING

Disillusioned, Siddharta sat at the foot of a tree near Gaya (now in Bihar, India) on the bank of the river. He resolved to sit there in meditation until he found his heart's desire. He sat like this for four weeks. During this time he experienced an intense spiritual opposition, which Buddhist tradition describes as the tempter Mara, literally, 'the Killer'. Later traditions have embroidered this experience with images of lustful women floating by and demons trying to attack him. Gradually, through the night, step by step, he began to see things differently, and the evil visions ceased.

He met the dawn as a Buddha, an Enlightened One. He stayed for a while, unsure that he could communicate what he had seen. Only one who becomes enlightened can see this. He eventually felt that he could explain enough and give people the steps to take towards this.

According to later Buddhist Scriptures, he had a vision of everything he had experienced throughout his many previous lives. He saw millions of creatures being born and dying like a great wheel. Then he saw how to make this stop, how to tackle the craving that made people grasp onto things that were

A painting of the Buddha sleeping.

Types of Buddhism

The earliest form of Buddhism spread through India, Sri Lanka, Thailand and other parts of South East Asia. This is known as Theravada Buddhism, meaning 'way of the elders', following what are believed to be the earliest teachings. Mahayana Buddhism is 'the greater vehicle' as practised in places such as Tibet. This has added other ideas and sees Buddha as more than human, with a series of earlier Buddhas and later Buddhas who arise to help humanity. There are *Bodhisattvas*, people who attain enlightenment but who choose to remain in the flesh to teach and to help people. Compassion is a driving force in *Bodhisattva* belief. The Buddhas are not God or quite gods, though they come very close to this.

Like other faiths, Buddhism can have nominal followers and more devoted ones, and can develop aspects of syncretism in some cultures. An example of such would be the use of home shrines for ancestor worship, a 'pagan' practice that predated the arrival of Buddhism to their shores.

'Where no thing is, where no grasping is, that is the isle of the no-beyond, *nibbana*, where decay and death are no more; this I declare to you.'

The Buddha,
the **Sutta Nipata**

'The royal chariots wear out, and so too the body ages. The true *dharma* does not age.'

The Buddha, the Pali Canon

'This *dharma* I teach is deep, difficult to see, difficult to understand, peaceful, excellent, beyond dialectic, subtle, intelligible to the wise.'

The Buddha, the Pali Canon

❈

Nirvana

Nirvana (*nibbana* in Pali) is another version of the goal, the Buddhist heaven. This comes from the word meaning 'to cool', and to be in a state of *nirvana* is like stepping out of the noonday sun into the shade. It is to be cooled of the heat of the passions, to let go and be at peace. The Western slang 'Cool!', meaning something that is really good, derives from Buddhism via the Beat generation of the 1950s and early 1960s.

The Buddha spoke usually about the cool person, one who has attained the state of *nirvana*, or the one who is *nibbuta* in the Pali texts. The *nibbuta* person has died to the illusion of self. This can be referred to as *kilesa nibbana*, the dying away of moral defilement, and *khanda nibbana*, the death of the body and the empirical self. The *nibbuta* person can go on living as a teacher and as an example, but he or she is free to depart from the Wheel of Life at any moment.

Buddhist texts describe *nirvana/nibbana* in a variety of ways. It cannot be imagined and is not a place as such. It is a state of being, a condition. It is a deep moral change and purification characterized by three things: *sunnata*, *apranihita* and *animita*.

Sunnata means 'void', an emptiness without form; *apranihita* means 'contentment' and not craving; *animita* means 'non-conceptual' – one cannot imagine *nirvana/nibbana*.

There is also a transcendental dimension to *nirvana/nibbana*. This might be less obvious in the texts as Buddhism is so 'this worldly' and practical, but it is there. It is called 'the beyond', *paramam*. It is taught that those who recognize this are 'exceedingly cooled', *abhinibbuta*.

impermanent and the suffering that resulted. He saw that the mind was not a fixed entity but constantly changing, part of a greater whole. Everything in the world is the result of causes and changes, including the 'I' inside our heads. The pipal tree was then known as the Bodhi tree, from the root word meaning 'enlightenment' or 'awakening'. This is sometimes shortened to the Bo tree.

THE PATH

Gautama Buddha is often called 'the Buddha' as he is seen as the first by Buddhists, but he is not unique in their eyes. Anyone can become a Buddha if they make the right spiritual progression. There is a spark of something inside everyone, an aptitude, an ability, to reach those heights.

The Goal

'As cool water allays feverish heat, so also nirvana removes the craving for sensuous enjoyments, the craving for further becoming, the cessation of becoming.'

The Buddha, the Pali Canon

DHARMA

Buddhism does not have a God. There are various gods mentioned in early Buddhist texts, such as the evil god Mara or some of the Vedic gods. There is a certain ambivalence shown towards them, and it has been suggested that they were part of the celestial, mythological scenery but were not active powers for the early Buddhists. Buddha taught *dharma* (Sanskrit) or *dhamma* (Pali). This term can be given several different meanings according to scholars, but it is fundamentally that which binds all things together, the only thing that is self-subsistent. It is 'the Way', 'the Law', 'the Teaching', 'the Truth' and 'the Life Force'. It is akin to the *Logos* (Word) in ancient Greek philosophy and early Christianity, the 'reason' that holds things in being. Asian Christians translate 'the Word' from John's Gospel in the Bible as *dharma*, for example. Total union with *dharma*, living life in the flow of it, is one version of the Buddhist goal.

THE *ANATMAN*

Buddha taught that there is no permanent self or fixed immortal soul in a person. The self is a construct of many influences and forces and is constantly in flux; it has no boundaries and only *dharma* or the state of *nirvana* is eternal. *Anatman* meant 'no soul' as against the Hindu teaching of the spark of the divine that resides in everyone, the *atman*. There is consciousness, though, something mysterious and precious that has evolved in human beings, and this cluster of psychic forces can be reborn again and again until it is pure.

The self can be analyzed as the five 'heaps', *Khandhas*, which comprise the physical body, sensation, perception, volition or will and consciousness. Together, they form an illusion of an enduring reality, but they can be broken apart.

ANOTHER WAY OF SAYING 'GOD'?

Some wonder if the Buddhist teachings are speaking of something similar to what other believers call 'God' but from an impersonal perspective. The Buddha did teach that there was that which is eternal and unchanging, without form. Buddhism tends to understand the concept of God as a force or a person over and above an individual, a huge Ego that commands the little ego. It is a tyranny, and Buddhism throws the individual back on themselves. The truth is within them and not above them. There is no one to pray to (Buddhists do not pray to Buddha). In Buddhism we all have a true self, imagined as a pearl, which is obscured by layers of wrong feelings and choices, illusions of craving and selfishness. The aim is to get in touch with the pearl within and seek to cleanse it.

No doubt some forms of belief in God or gods are destructive and infantile, based upon fear and domination. It would be ridiculous to reject all theism as such, of course, and there is sublime, non-conceptual, spiritual teaching about the reality of God and the soul's relation to God that might not be a million miles away from all that Buddhists really hold dear. Here, there is room for dialogue. After all, Buddhists recognize that the ego is not fixed and supreme; they need to open up to *dharma* that existed before them. Theists know that they are not alone but have to open up to the reality of God. When asking a Buddhist, 'Might there not be God along the Way and at the end of the Way?' I usually get the reply, 'Why bother with the question? Just follow the Way!' The Buddha set aside metaphysics as a distraction from the true path. He told the story of a man who was shot by an arrow. When someone came to help him, he did not ask first 'Who did this to me?' but cried 'Just pull it out!'

Teachers of the Way

'*What use is there for a well if water is everywhere? When craving's root is severed what should one go about seeking?*'

The Buddha, the Pali Canon

THE BUDDHA

The Buddha saw himself as a type but not as a unique person. What he had found, others could too. A story was told about offerings. The Buddha was preaching to a Hindu Brahmin priest. The Buddha spoke of the *nibbuta* person, cooled from harmful desires. It is he or she who is worthy of offerings. The

Brahmin offered a sacred cake to the Buddha in respect, but it was refused. The Brahmin was upset and confused. He asked again who was worthy to receive offerings. The Buddha spoke again of the one who is *nibbuta*. 'But who else is this but you, O Buddha, most worthy recipient of all the world as an offering!' The Buddha only accepts this *nibbuta* person as a type, as an ideal, and not as a particular individual. Others can follow him. One recent book about Buddhism was called *If You Meet Buddha on the Road, Kill Him*, showing that Buddha is a help to wholeness and not a God. The truth is within each person.

OTHER BUDDHAS

Mahayana Buddhism tends to honour other teachers with the title 'Buddha' such as Amida Buddha who founded the Pure Land movement or the *Bodhisattvas*, the enlightened individuals who chose to return to earth to help others in various ways. Avalokiteshvara, the Buddha of Compassion, is one such, either pictured as descending a mountain or sitting in peaceful meditation with many arms radiating outwards to help. Some Mahayana Buddhists look forward to the coming of a final Buddha, Maitreya, 'the loving one'.

SCRIPTURES

The first Buddhist Scriptures were written down several hundred years after the death of the Buddha. There was a long oral tradition. The first writings were on palm leaves threaded together with a board laid on top to keep them flat. Today, some Scriptures are still produced like this, beautifully illustrated and wrapped in cloths to protect them.

Others are printed in the form of modern books. The earliest books were written in Pali and were collected in the first century CE. These are the *Tripitaka*, the 'Three Baskets', also known as the Pali Canon. These comprised three different collections:

- ❀ *Vinaya-pitaka* – rules for monks and nuns
- ❀ *Sutta-pitaka* – five collections of the teaching of the Buddha
- ❀ *Abhidhamma-pitaka* – Buddhist philosophical texts.

Buddhists regard the *Sutta-pitaka* as the most important as this is from the Buddha himself. A core test here is the *Dhammapada*, 'The Way of the Teaching'. A curious collection in the *Sutta-pitaka* are the Jataka Tales. These are what modern people would call a 'prequel' for they detail previous lives of the Buddha, either as human or animal. One such tale is of the Monkey King who led his people to safety across a ravine by lying down to make himself into a bridge. His back broke under the strain and he fell to his death, selflessly.

Mahayana Buddhists have extra Scriptures called the *Sutras,* which they believe to be more hidden, oral teachings of the Buddha that they have retained. Tibetan Buddhists learn the Scriptures by forming pairs and holding a debate. One makes a statement and the other argues against it. This tests their knowledge.

Some Buddhists still rely more on oral traditions, such as the Zen Buddhists who have rituals and sayings that are handed down from teacher to teacher. This form of Buddhism originated in the sixth century CE, when missionaries came to India from China. It has also taken root in Japan.

THE *SANGHA*

The *sangha* is the community. This is the whole Buddhist community and Buddhists believe that they need other Buddhists to help them follow *dharma*. The *sangha* was originally the monks and nuns. When Buddha was first preaching, his followers travelled around in the cooler and dryer seasons teaching, and

Devotees honour Buddhist monks by offering food.

they gathered together in resting places called *viharas* in the wet season. This followed the pattern of Hindu *sadhus* who would gather for mutual support in adverse weather. Gradually, the *viharas* became permanent with monks living in them all year round, and rules of life were drawn up.

Buddhist monks are called *bhikhus* and they practise renunciation, having only a saffron robe and a wooden bowl. They receive offerings from passers-by and live off these. This teaches them dependency on others and humility. Later, women were admitted as *bhikhunis* and special communities were set up for them. The Buddha was radical in his choice of *bhikhus* for he rejected the Indian caste system with its social classes of priests, warriors, merchants and workers. Any caste member could join, and this was a liberating affair, as it was for women to be seen as equals in following *dharma*.

In Buddhist countries, some young men and women become *bhikhus* for a time as part of their training for life.

Treasury of the Heart

'Hate is not conquered by hate: hate is conquered by love. This is a law eternal.'

The Buddha, The *Dhammapada*

THE FOUR NOBLE TRUTHS
The Buddha's first sermon was at Sarnath near Banaras. This is known as 'the Fire Sermon' for he declared that all the world is on fire with cravings and passions. He outlined the Four Noble

The Noble Eightfold Path

The Buddha taught a set of eight precepts to guide people through the Middle Way:
1. Right view – understand the Four Noble Truths.
2. Right intention – be committed to the path.
3. Right speech – always speak the truth and be positive.
4. Right action – be kind to all living things and be clear minded.
5. Right livelihood – earn your living ethically.
6. Right effort – avoid harmful thoughts.
7. Right mindfulness – live in reality and be aware of people around you.
8. Right contemplation – train the mind to be free from hatred and greed.

These are seen as a series of steps. The first two tell Buddhists to take the teaching seriously; the next three are about how we act; the last three are about training the mind.

Truths in the form of a medical examination of his day with a statement of the problem and a prescription of a remedy:
1. *Dukkha* ('Suffering') – all life involves suffering
2. Craving – the origin of *dukkha* is craving, false attachments
3. Cessation – the cure for *dukkha* is to stop craving the wrong thing
4. The Middle Way – Buddha had known luxury and asceticism. Neither brought happiness and so he taught the Middle Way, a way of avoiding extremes.

THREE UNIVERSAL TRUTHS

1. The Buddha taught change, *anicca*. Everything changes constantly and is interrelated. Existence is social, not individual. A butterfly's wings flapping in the East are linked to a tempest in the West. From the tiniest atom to the largest galaxies, existence is dependent. Life depends on certain conditions such as sunlight and water. Remove these and life disappears. Certain forces come into play, and things emerge; life exists or vanishes.

2. The Buddha taught that there is no permanent self, *anatta*. Our consciousness is real but always changing, and it is linked to all other life. There are no clear boundaries.

3. The Buddha taught suffering, *dukkha*. Cravings come from insecurity and a lack of contentment. We seek more things, and life cannot make people completely happy.

THE PATH AS A GUIDE

The Eightfold Path is not a belief but a practical guide. Buddhists have few beliefs as such. They do not have to believe the Path will work, they merely have to try it and keep on going. They might believe in *nirvana* as a goal, although no one can experience this until they are there, but they can walk along the path of *dharma* and see its benefits at work within them. The Buddha taught that all things are as they are because of external conditions. A seed is planted and watered, the sun shines and it grows. Give people the right conditions, the right input and disciples, and they will grow spiritually and morally.

THE WHEEL OF LIFE

One of the beliefs of Buddhism is the round of rebirths, *samsara*. The world is seen as illusion, *maya*, in the sense that this is impermanent, just as in Hinduism, a person's actions generate *karma*, which affects how they are reborn. Your five senses grasp what they perceive and you become one with them – desire is translated into action. *Karma* results. Although there is no permanent soul, the consciousness is reincarnated time and time again, growing and changing as a result. Liberation comes with enlightenment and entry into the cooled state of *nirvana*.

The Buddhist depiction of the Wheel of Life shows various levels of reality and changing states around it, with the god of death holding it in his grip. Above this figure, the Buddha points the way, and a hare leaps in the moon, an image of enlightenment.

Right mindfulness

Buddhists have meditation exercises that help them to calm themselves and to focus. One exercise helps them to value the present moment. They sit quietly and still, breathing in a steady rhythm for a while. Then they imagine that they are on a warm, sandy beach. They take one step and feel the soft, warm sand beneath their feet. They walk on, step by step, putting worries behind them and attending to the present moment with each step.

'Watchfulness is the path of immortality; unwatchfulness is the path of death. Those who are watchful never die: those who do not watch are already dead.'
The Buddha, the Pali Canon

'There is an unborn, un-become, unmade, incomposite, and were there not, there would be no escape from the born, the become, the made and the composite world.'
The Buddha, the Pali Canon

'Buddhist teachings help me to focus, to clear my mind of rubbish and to calm my emotions. It is wise teaching.'
A Buddhist nun in Sri Lanka

✳

Following spread:
The Wheel of Rebirth.

Paths to Peace

'Deeds done in harmony with one's path of life are those which bring clarity and peace and harmony to the doer.'

The Buddha, the Pali Canon

SAMATHA

The basic level of meditation for Buddhists is *samatha*. This is a series of exercises involving posture, breathing, and focusing of the mind. The lotus position has the back straight, the legs crossed and the hands resting in the lap, gently connected. Breathing exercises vary, but the aim is to slow the breathing slightly and create a regular rhythm. There is an attempt to focus, and this might be by directing the breath to the tip of the nose. Or it might involve listening to sounds that are far away for a time, and then switching to ones close by. This switches back and forwards until people can sense their own heartbeat. A simple visualization then takes place. One might imagine a peaceful place, or an object, or an idea such as 'peace' held in the consciousness.

This centres a person down and calms them. Buddhists claim that when they advance in this method and spend enough time doing it, they have various pleasant sensations such as feeling joy well up like water bubbling up from a spring, or being enveloped in a white cloak. This is a way of letting go and of de-stressing the self.

A calm lake suggests a state of inner peace and tranquillity.

COMPASSION

One meditation technique involves imagining people they love and care for. Then people who annoy them, or whom they are wary of, come into mind. The meditator tries to imagine them changing, their feelings towards them changing into compassion or *metta*. Going deeper, feelings of *metta* will radiate out to all around. This helps to raise the consciousness to cope better with difficult people. One key point of the Buddhist Way is to perceive things differently, to change how the mind thinks. The goal is to become enlightened through meditation, *Samadhi*.

VIPASSANA

Vipassana means 'insight' meditation and it is far more advanced than *samatha*. It is only recommended to people experienced in meditation and under the guidance of a teacher. The teacher will guide and suggest, like a doctor giving a prescription. In fact, it is thought that this level of meditation can be dangerous to the uninitiated. It works by visualizing an object and thinking through the changes that occur within it. Thus flowers can be visualized, and their gradual decay focused upon. Or a scene of death can be the visualized, recalling the transience of our lives. It jolts people 'awake' spiritually, reminding them of limitations and mortality. Humans are just part of a much, much bigger whole. This can help people put their problems into perspective.

BRAIN WAVES

Waking consciousness is made up of beta waves. Sleep involves alpha waves and

 Mantras and mandalas

Some branches of Buddhism, in particular types of Mahayana practised in Tibet and Japan, use *mantras*, phrases which are repeated over and over again as chants. These will be in Pali or Sanskrit. The most famous is *om mani padme hum*, known as 'the jewel in the lotus'.

Chanting teaches right concentration and it is thought that the sacred chant gives off vibrations that open up new levels of consciousness. Flicking books of the Scriptures is also thought to give off such energy, as are Tibetan prayer wheels, which have *mantras* inscribed upon them.

Tibetan monks create elaborate *mandalas* in coloured sand. A *mandala* has four points that balance each other, representing aspects of the mind or emotions. The patterns are made in sand so that they will not last. Focusing the mind to make them and showing reverence to them is balanced by their temporariness as they are blown away later on. It is a therapeutic discipline to put into practice Buddhist precepts.

Zen Buddhism uses other rituals in this way, including a tea-drinking ceremony and flower arranging.

delta when entering deep sleep. The mental state of a person meditating is apparently like that of the early stages of sleep, using alpha waves. On the fringes of slumber, we can easily imagine things and images can pop into our minds. It can be highly creative.

THE FIVE PRECEPTS

Meditation seeks to help Buddhists to

calm the mind and to follow *dharma*. The Five Precepts are a set of simple guidelines for behaviour.

1. I will avoid taking life.
2. I will avoid taking what is not given.
3. I will avoid harmful sexual activity.
4. I will avoid saying what is not true.
5. I will avoid clouding my mind with alcohol or drugs.

Awe and Wonder

> *'Drench, pervade, fill and pervade this body itself with zest and ease that are born of contemplation.'*
>
> The Buddha, the Pali Canon

TAKING REFUGE

Buddhists speak of 'taking refuge', by going to a safe place in the teachings of the Buddha and by belonging to the community of Buddhists. The Three Jewels are expressions of this safety:

> *'I go to the Buddha for refuge.*
> *I go to the* dharma
> *for refuge.*
> *I go to the* Sangha *for refuge.'*

Buddhists may bow down three times, reciting the Three Jewels, when they enter a shrine. They may make three small offerings of a candle, a flower and incense. The candle represents enlightenment; the flower represents beauty and the inevitability of decay; the incense is the aroma of virtue.

SHRINES AND *VIHARAS*

A shrine can be in a corner of a room in a private house, or in a room in a hall, a *vihara,* or attached to a monastery.

A shrine in a *vihara* will have certain features such as:

✿ an image of the Buddha
✿ offering bowls – usually seven bowls of water before the image as a symbol of welcome. Just as a visitor would be offered water to drink, these bowls are there to welcome the Buddha.
✿ flowers, candles and incense
✿ a small bell or gong to warn people that chanting or meditation is about to begin
✿ perhaps colourful embroidered images of the Buddha and the *Bodhisattvas* hung on the walls.

Buddhist worship is called *puja*, as in Hinduism. Here, the Buddhist will make three prostrations before the image and make the traditional offerings. The image is not worshipped as such; the person is bowing to what it represents, the Buddha, but it is honoured as though he is there. The prostrations remind the worshipper that they are totally dependent upon the Buddha and *dharma*. Remember that the Buddha is not a god; it is his enlightenment and teaching that are honoured rather than the Buddha himself. There will then be the reading and chanting of Scriptures or *mantras*.

A shrine room in a home will be much simpler, with a small image and incense sticks. Buddhists will normally bow and put their hands together in greeting when entering their shrine room.

There are no rules about how often a person should make a *puja* and visit a shrine. Some do so rarely, at festivals only, and some regularly. *Puja* can be made at home, and a Buddhist can meditate anywhere.

STUPAS

Stupas are special monuments that contain relics of the Buddha. He died from eating poisonous mushrooms and he was cremated. His ashes were sent to various places and *stupas* were built on these. A famous one is at Kandy where one of Buddha's teeth is kept. These monuments are called *stupas* in India and *dagobas* in Sri Lanka. They are dome-shaped buildings that are solidly built. They are found in the grounds of *viharas* and pilgrims walk around them to show respect. The whole worship area is called by different names such as *wats* in Thailand, *pagodas* in Burma and *chortens* in Tibet.

There are usually smaller shrines around the grounds. These will have different designs according to the country. In Thailand, for example, they are bell-shaped and highly decorated.

IMAGES OF THE BUDDHA

Images of the Buddha follow a pattern of symbolism. His head will have a flame coming out of it or a bump (an extra brain) to show his enlightenment and wisdom. His earlobes will be long as this was the custom for holy men at the time. If the image shows the Buddha teaching, then the hands will be depicted in a certain way, and in other ways for meditation or for fearlessness, calmness or generosity. Mahayana shrines can have images of *Bodhisattvas* and some of these are of women such as Manjugosha, who holds a flaming sword of wisdom that cuts through ignorance, or Tara, who is shown descending from her lotus throne.

Tibetan Buddhism has a rich array of exotic images, which might seem frightening or strange to an outsider.

Wrathful images show a Buddha with a monstrous face surrounded by skulls with a sword in his hand. This represents the powerful emotion behind anger, which, left unguided, becomes destructive, but can be transformed into positive energy to fight against injustice and ignorance. A more surprising image is sexual in tone. A *Yab-Yum* image represents a mother–father relationship. This seems erotic, even pornographic by Western

A Buddhist stupa, containing relics of the Buddha.

standards, but it is a symbol of two complementary forces joining in a harmony, of wisdom and compassion working together.

VAJRA

Sometimes Tibetan Buddhists will hold a symbol called a *vajra*. (This design in Hinduism can represent a diamond and a flash of lightning at the same time.) Tibetan Buddhists sometimes hold a bell in their left hand, which represents wisdom; and a *vajra* in their right hand, which represents skill and compassion.

MALA

Buddhists in Nepal and Tibet use prayer beads called *mala*. These can have 108, 54 or 27 beads. These are used to count the number of prostrations before a Buddha image, and a *mantra* or a name of a Buddha is recited on each bead. Sometimes there are three larger beads, representing the Three Jewels of the Buddha, *dharma* and the *Sangha*.

Journey into Mystery

'It is better to spend one day contemplating the birth and death of all things than a hundred years never contemplating beginnings and endings.'

The Buddha, the Pali Canon

THE LOTUS FLOWER

The lotus flower is one of the main Buddhist symbols because it is something beautiful that grows out of the mud. It represents enlightenment coming to a mind clouded by passions and cravings. Hence the meditation posture is known as the lotus position, and during worship a Buddhist might cup their hands together to represent a lotus flower.

EMPTY SPACES

The French philosopher Roland Barthes (1915–80) wrote a series of articles on modern icons of sport, fashion and consumerism in his 'Mythologies' in the

The lotus flower opens up to the light – a symbol of enlightenment.

1950s. He was fascinated by the image of the Eiffel Tower, reaching up tall against the Parisian landscape. It was largely made up of empty spaces, girder patterns criss-crossing with huge sections of open air. As he put it, 'Its form is empty but present, its meaning absent but full.'

Negative spaces are vital ingredients in paintings, photographs and in our own perception of reality. They act as frames for substance. The very lack allows something else to be, to take form and shape before our eyes. Buddhism uses the concept of emptiness in a similar manner.

Emptiness is letting go; emptiness is non-discursive reasoning; emptiness is humility; emptiness is patience and waiting. Emptying the mind of harmful thoughts is not to create a blankness, but a clean place where creativity and compassion can bubble up.

Emptiness also opens up the reality of non-permanence. The self is a combination of the five heaps or *khandas*, which make up an illusory whole; the ego is a stream of consciousness with no fixed point. Even the very atoms that a person can be reduced down to are seen to be in flux, impermanent and changing.

Buddhism deals in philosophy more than other faiths. It has few beliefs but many concepts. It often likes to tease. Apparently, when Buddhism first reached China in the first century CE, the emperor asked a *bhikhu*:

'What is the first principle of Buddhism?'
The answer came, 'Vast emptiness.'
The emperor replied, 'Who then am I speaking to?'
'I have no idea,' said the bhikhu.

The *koan* and *haiku*

The *Koan*
Zen Buddhism uses teasing phrases to open up the mind. A Zen master will give a pupil a particular *koan* to meditate upon. Common ones are 'What is the sound of one hand clapping?', or when one Buddhist pupil asked if a dog had a Buddha-nature within. The Master replied *Mu!* (meaning 'No!') but he barked it like a dog.

Another concerns a goose trapped in a bottle. You cannot get it out without breaking the glass. What do you do? A Master rose to his feet, clapped his hands and said, 'There! It's out!'

A further example is of a Zen Master who was walking one day with a pupil, and saw some trees on the horizon. 'Look, Master!' said the pupil. 'What excellent firewood they would make!'

The Master looked and said softly, 'I can only see beautiful trees.'

Koans are about thinking the impossible, daring to be different, original and unique.

Haiku
Zen also uses simple poetry to tease the mind open. *Haikus* are three-line poems that dwell upon feelings or things in nature. Seeing the beauty of nature is intrinsic to right mindfulness for Buddhism, as well as a way of cultivating compassion. A *haiku* might be:

'A frog on the lily pad,
the sunlight dancing,
the ripple in the pond as it was gone.'

The concept of the Void stands for the empty space that allows the universe to be. It is mystery, not-knowing.

CANDLE FLAMES

Buddhists believe in the mystery of rebirth. The consciousness lives on in another life, rather as one candle can be lit by the flame of another. The former is extinguished, but the new one burns on. Some forms of Buddhism teach that it is very unlikely that a person will be reborn as a human. They tell a parable. Imagine that a blind turtle swims in the ocean and surfaces once every hundred years. A golden ring floats on the surface of the ocean somewhere. What are the chances that the turtle will surface with its neck in this ring?

This gloomy picture stresses how precious human life is.

THE DALAI LAMA

A belief developed in Tibetan Buddhism that the successor to the Dalai Lama, their spiritual leader, can be chosen by a series of tests. A boy can be chosen as the reincarnated Dalai Lama from these, partly by recognizing the deceased Dalai

The Dalai Lama.

Lama's belongings. This is unusual in Buddhism as most people have no recollection of their previous lives. Only advanced Masters, practised in truth meditation, might claim such insight. This custom, known as *tulku*, was unknown until the twelfth century CE and was formulated because of a dynastic dispute. The present Dalai Lama has expressed a desire to move to an elective system after his death, and he feels that some of his selection tests were passed by sheer good fortune!

Making Merry

Even as the moon makes light in black darkness, even so in one moment the supreme bliss removes all defilements.'
The Buddha, the Pali Canon

FEW FESTIVALS

Buddhism does not have many festivals to its name. There are no rules concerning the festivals and how they should be celebrated. The Buddha taught people not to trust too much in religious ceremonies, but to follow an inner path of *dharma*. Celebrating a festival is an opportunity for sharing and enjoyment, for working together in a spirit of cooperation and for learning some teachings about the Buddha. There is only one main festival concerning Gautama. Perhaps this is because for the Buddha it was important to walk on in the path and not constantly look back.

Birth of the Buddha

There are numerous legends of the Buddha's childhood which were written down several hundred years after his death. There is a birth story that says that his mother Maya dreamed of a white elephant that entered her womb. Ten months later she gave birth as the earth trembled during a full moon in May. Maya died seven months later; the tradition teaches that anyone who has borne a Buddha has no other purpose in life. Siddharta was then brought up by an aunt. Note the mention of the full moon, and thus the connection of his birth celebrations at *Wesak*.

WESAK

Wesak celebrates the Buddha's birth. This is the most important Buddhist festival and is celebrated at full moon in May. It focuses on the birth of the Buddha but also remembers his enlightenment and death. Local customs will vary, but there are often colourful processions and decorations in the shrines. Homes will be filled with candles in some places. The candle is a symbol of enlightenment, of the truth of *dharma*.

BUTTER AND SAND

Tibetan Buddhists celebrate their festivals with much colour and dancing. They wear costumes and blow ceremonial horns. A striking feature of their celebrations is the making of temporary images of butter or coloured sand. These are done with great dedication and reverence, despite knowing that they will melt or be blown away. They teach that life is constantly moving and impermanent.

NEW YEAR

Some Buddhist countries celebrate a New Year festival. The date will vary from country to country. In Thailand, for example, this is in April and it is called Songkran Day. Water is a central symbol for this day. Water symbolizes life and cleansing, and people splash it joyfully over each other in a party atmosphere. Images of the Buddha will be ceremonially washed clean at this time too. There is a practice that seeks to save and affirm life, and to store up good *karma* for the Buddhist. Fish and eels are rescued from dried-up areas and released into rivers. This helps the creature on whom the person is having compassion and gains merit for them. Birds can also be let out of cages.

FULL MOON

In many Buddhist countries the full moon is celebrated each month. The light of the moon appearing in the night sky is an image of enlightenment. Just as the moonlight dispels the darkness, so when a person awakens to their Buddha nature and *dharma*, darkness goes from their mind. The moon is one symbol for Enlightenment in Buddhism. Festival days associated with the moon are called *Uposatha* days, when new clothes might be worn.

TEACHING *DHARMA*

Many Buddhists also celebrate the time when the Buddha first began to teach *dharma* at Sarnath, giving his Fire Sermon and revealing the Four Noble Truths.

'With this lamp which blazes with firm strength, destroying darkness, I make offering to the truly enlightened lamp of the world, the dispeller of darkness…'
Prayer for ***Wesak*** Day

'Water fights at New Year are great fun. We try to get as many people as possible, especially the adults and our teachers!'
Buddhist youth from Thailand

Buddhist monks create a mandala from coloured sand.

OTHER FESTIVALS

Famous teachers can also be remembered, such as the *Bodhisattvas* or sages such as Padmasambhava, the first *bhikhu* to bring Buddhism to Tibet.

KATHINA

The first Buddhist *bhikhus* used to meet together and study during the months of the rainy season when it was difficult to travel. The custom of *bhikhus* having a retreat at this time of the autumn has carried on, and Buddhists come to give them gifts. They will sit in rows with their bowls to receive these. This is the *Kathina*.

Today

'The end remains untold.'

The Buddha, the Pali Canon

WESTERN PHILOSOPHY LOOKS EAST

Buddhism's interest in Eastern philosophy and its idea of constant change and impermanence lends itself to Western postmodernist thought. Postmodernism, which has arisen since the end of the Second World War, largely in France, is teasing and playful also. The power of the imagination and the emotions is tapped into as well as

Western Buddhism

With travel to the Far East having become more frequent and easy, Buddhism is attractive to many Western travellers. Buddhist *bhikhus* have also travelled West to teach converts. Examples include the Tibetan Chogyam Trungpa who fled from the communists in 1959 to India and eventually co-founded the first Tibetan monastery in the West in Dumfriesshire in Scotland. He was the first Tibetan to be given a British passport. Later, he gave up being a monk, married and moved to the USA where he founded retreat centres, a Buddhist University and monasteries. He was a close friend of the beat poet Allen Ginsberg. Some of his advanced meditation students were taught to meditate on the word 'Be!' for at least half an hour a day and he was frustrated that Westerners found it hard to simply 'be'. Some of the teachers who travel West are colourful characters, and, sadly, they have not always been free of scandal and there have been accusations of sexual liaisons with students.

One humorous anecdote suggests how the Western Buddhists need to relax and be themselves rather than trying to emulate foreign cultures in their zeal to be authentically Buddhist. A Master died and his students tried to preserve his body in meditation position by packing it with salt. They had to constantly renew the salt to keep it clean, an exhausting process. When a lama came from Tibet to attend the funerary rites, he looked at them in exasperation: 'Don't you know about deep freezers in the West?'

Zen Buddhism has also taken root successfully in the West, and the Western Buddhist order seeks to adapt Buddhism to a new culture and set of needs. Beliefs vary, and some Westerns are reverently agnostic about things like reincarnation. They seek to meditate, clear the mind, and to have ethics to live by. This type of Buddhism is proving very popular with people fed up with materialism but who are spiritually uncertain and adrift from traditional faiths. They do not have to believe very much, but they can do many things. Particularly in the USA, Buddhism attracts movie stars and celebrities such as Richard Gere, and it is one of the fastest growing types of faith.

discursive reason. Poetry and abstract art can speak of the sublime, of depths that reason cannot.

The limitations of human knowledge are stressed by postmodernism, as we are conditioned by time and culture. Metaphysics is dismissed as 'foundationalism', an attempt to underpin reality with a God or system when we have no sure knowledge of what lies beyond human discourse and this world. The self is seen as a social construct in the works of the psychoanalyst Jacques Lacan: identity is created by language. We are what we say we are. Everything is changing, fads and fashions come and go, and there are no metanarratives or grand theories of life, the universe and everything. These theories and systems – whether religious, scientific, political or philosophical – are rejected. Instead, there are many little stories and local ideas; the bigger picture eludes our grasp.

Postmodernist thinkers pick away at concepts and systems, deconstructing them into their component parts and influences, searching through their

伏馴

The disciple herding the ox – a symbol of the unenlightened mind.

historical development and tracing the 'archeology of ideas'. They point out how images – simulations of reality – are much used in modern media and discourse. They toy with ideas of emptiness and use the Eastern term 'the void'. There is that which cannot be spoken, but it can begin to be felt.

Buddhism chimes in with much of the above, although it does teach the reality of eternal *dharma* and a state or condition of *nirvana* that can be entered, freeing one of the constant change. Western Buddhist Stephen Batchelor argues that Buddhism is like a series of postmodern *koans*, and he points to the work of Narajuna (second century CE), which urges people to move on and let go.

The ancient wisdom of Buddhism has found fertile ground in some Western philosophy today.

POLITICS

Some Buddhist countries have suffered under communism in the twentieth and early twenty-first centuries. Tibet was annexed by China in the 1950s, and many monasteries have been closed, perhaps as many as 6,000. About 100,000 Tibetans have fled to India, including the present Dalai Lama. Treating Tibet as an 'autonomous region' has led to much resettlement by ethnic Chinese and the teaching of the Chinese language only. The completion of rail links has speeded up the process and much traditional culture has been lost. Mongolia became communist in 1924, and novice *bhikhus* were allowed to train only as late as 1980. Buddhism is flourishing again in northern China.

THE BOY AND THE OX

A fitting way to sum up Buddhism is the series of drawings in China and Japan of a boy searching for his lost ox. These are within circles. There is a search, clues, a chase and eventually the beast is tamed. Then the boy walks back to the marketplace, happy. The closing circles show the ox as invisible and the beauty of the world around. One is empty, symbolizing *nirvana*. The boy has entered the state of enlightenment through meditation, *samadhi*. The ox represents *karma* and the struggle with the ego.

> 'Buddhism is practical and not about believing impossible, unprovable things. It is a way to work on the mind, to better the self.'
> Russell, a Western Buddhist from London
>
> ✳

| BUDDHISM | at a glance... |

- When did it begin? – the sixth century BCE in India.
- The founder – Siddharta Gautama (c. 563–483 BCE) of the Shakyamuni clan in northern India. He was a prince who renounced wife and child to live as a holy man in the forest.
- God – The Buddha placed *dharma* (Way) above the gods; Buddhism is agnostic but teaches a spiritual path, seeking enlightenment and the bliss of *nirvana*.
- Redeemer figure – Buddha is a teacher and no more. His example should set people searching for the 'Buddha nature' within them.
- Scriptures – Various writings of the Buddha or the early sages are compiled in the *Tripitaka* (the 'Three Baskets'). The *Dhammapada* is a popular, short collection of wise sayings of the Buddha.
- Beliefs – There is a cycle of rebirth and the soul only escapes this by detachment from all that causes suffering. This means that many rebirths may be necessary. Buddha taught the Middle Way, avoiding both extreme asceticism and laxity. Each person can achieve enlightenment; the potential is there within them. *Nirvana* is the state of being 'cooled' from desires, free and at peace.
- Place of worship – Buddhists can meditate and honour the Buddha in home shrines or in *viharas*. These are public prayer halls that contain a statue of the Buddha. Monasteries also have meditation rooms.
- Sacred food – Buddhists seek to avoid eating meat, though this is allowed, particularly in situations when other food is scarce.
- Main festivals – *Wesak* celebrates the birth of the Buddha. *Uposatha* days celebrate phases of the moon.
- Key symbols – the wheel of rebirth; the footprint of the Buddha suggests that life is a journey to enlightenment.

Sikhism

'In this dish are placed three things: truth, contentment, and wisdom, as well as the sweetness of God's name which is the support of everyone. Those who absorb and enjoy it shall be saved...'

Guru Granth Sahib

A LATECOMER

Sikhism is one of the newer world faiths, beginning in 1499 with the mystical experience of Nanak in an area of North India that is now Pakistan. It went through various developments during the lifetimes of its ten Gurus and began as a honest attempt to combine the best of Hinduism and Islam, to seek reconciliation and the worship of one God. Sikhs have lived integrally with Indian society for many years, sharing some Hindu festivals and having to use Hindu priests for marriage ceremonies in the early days.

As late as 1925, the Sikh Gurdwara Act was passed in India, trying to define who was a Sikh and who was not. This was thought to be too vague, and it was expanded upon in 1931.

THE LAND

The Punjab region of North India saw the origin and growth of the new faith, and the eventual establishment of a holy city, Amritsar, and a central place of worship, the Golden Temple. This region was ruled over by Muslim lords and Hindu kings at various times, and relationships with the Sikh community were not always easy. There were times of severe persecution. The Punjab is an area transected by five rivers (*panj* means five). It is a richly fertile zone, which various rulers and groups have sought to control.

In 1947, with the partition of India, the Punjab region was divided between India and Pakistan, and many Sikhs, about 2,600,000, moved into the Indian-controlled region. Though the main and ancestral homeland of the Sikhs, the Punjab is just part of the worldwide community. Sikhs have travelled throughout the world, especially the British empire as it then was. The largest community outside of the Punjab lives in Britain, where there are about 500,000. About 350,000 live in the USA.

In a nutshell

Sikhism, from the word *Sikh* meaning 'disciple' seeks to worship one God. Guru Nanak (1469–1539 CE) blended Islam and Hinduism into a new, original synthesis as he saw warring factions and bloodshed between the two great faiths. He chose his successor rather than allowing the title to pass down to his sons and thus form a dynasty. He chose his most trusted follower, and there was a succession of Gurus chosen by each successor in like manner. There were ten Gurus in all, and then the final Guru decreed that there would be no more living Gurus. Their holy book, the *Guru Granth Sahib*, would become the teacher of the people from then on. This had been assembled from hymns composed by the various Gurus as well as by Hindu and Muslim holy men.

The genius

Sikhism is a fresh, bold attempt to join two religions in one, remembering the importance of the heart and personal devotion to God.

The symbol

The Sikh symbol is a circle with swords. Swords are a symbol of truth as well as the right to self-defence. Sikhism has had to fight for its very existence at times. The two swords at each side reflect the two swords carried by the sixth Guru and they symbolize fighting for truth and for the spirit.

Guru Nanak teaching.

First Steps

'There is no Hindu, there is no Muslim, so whose path shall I follow? I shall follow God's path.'

Guru Nanak

GURU NANAK

Nanak's conversion came when he was 30. There are many stories told of his childhood leading up to this. These are collected in the *janam-sakhis*. He showed great insight into religious matters, for example, impressing Hindu priests and Muslim scholars.

He also was said to care for the poor, once giving away money his father had given him for business. (Nanak was born into a wealthy, high-caste Hindu family.) Then there were miracle stories, such as the time when a deadly cobra opened its hood to shade the sleeping boy Nanak from the sun, or the time when he was said to let cattle enter a neighbour's field. When the neighbour complained, the field was found to be undamaged, but the cattle apparently had had enough to eat.

Nanak always refused to accept any idea that he worked miracles; only the name of God could do that. Nanak saw himself as a teacher, a Guru.

Nanak married young, at about 18, and had two sons. Interestingly, he refused to carry out the Hindu ceremonies to purify and protect the children; he argued that birth was natural and a blessing, and that the only impurities were in the human mind and in our actions. His sister and brother-in-law found him a job working for a high-ranking Muslim where he worked until he was 30.

THE COURT OF HEAVEN

Nanak went to bathe one day in the river, and he said that he was taken up into the presence of God. This experience is known as entering the Court of Heaven. Nanak went missing for three days and the locals feared that he had drowned. Whether he was taken up physically or in the spirit is a mystery that is debated among Sikhs.

GOD IS EVERYWHERE

Once, Nanak lay down to sleep with his feet facing a holy place. The locals were outraged as this was seen as a great offence and insult. Nanak replied, 'But God lives everywhere!' Nanak frowned upon religious pilgrimage, as he taught that God could be found in all places, especially in the heart.

MILK AND BLOOD

Nanak would sometimes make dramatic gestures to back up his teachings. Once, he took a bowl of milk curd to a feast. He had received this from a poor carpenter. At the feast, he picked up a richer man's offering of meat; he squeezed first one and then the other. Out of the poor man's offering came milk, but out of the rich man's came blood. He made his point graphically. The rich man's offering came from the sweat and suffering of others.

THE NEXT GURU

Nanak chose his successor. He gave his two sons various menial tests such as carrying a pile of grass. They saw this as pointless and dirty work. A disciple, Lehna, carried it without complaining. Then Nanak dropped a coin into a pool of dirty water. The sons refused to get

Nanak's mission

Nanak went on four teaching journeys. He travelled to the Hindu holy places in India, as well as to Tibet and Sri Lanka. He also went to the Muslim holy places such as Makkah and those in Iraq and Iran. He travelled with a Muslim bard who set his teachings to music. In a non-literate age, people learnt by singing songs. Eventually, after about 20 years of travelling, he founded Kartarpur, in 1521. This was a town where Sikhs could live together and listen to his teachings. He invited all to sit and eat with him, opening a communal kitchen, or *langar*. This challenged the divisions of the caste system. He worked there with his family as a farmer until his death in 1539.

their hands dirty. Lehna pulled it out. Nanak thus chose his faithful disciple over his sons. He renamed Lehna 'Angad', meaning 'Myself'.

The Goal

> '*Without a Guru no one has reached God, for all his talking; it is he who shows the way and teaches the devotion.*'
>
> Guru Nanak

EK AUM-KAR

The above phrase means 'God is One' and can be used as a title or name of God by Sikhs. Guru Nanak spoke of the *Nam* and the *Sat Guru*. The *Nam* is the name of God and Sikhs chant this and meditate upon it. *Sat Guru* means 'true Guru'.

Guru Nanak disappeared for three days after going to bathe in the river. He claimed to have received a call from God at this time.

Nanak taught that God has no form; God is transcendent and mysterious, beyond. Nanak rejected the Hindu teaching about the appearances or *avatars* in which Vishnu took on the flesh of an animal or a human for a time in order to teach humanity. This is seen as unnecessary since God can speak into the human heart and through his Gurus. The word spoken by God into our hearts can guide and teach. We need no *avatars*. In this, Nanak was following Muslim belief very closely. For them, Allah is transcendent and cannot be compared to any created being.

THE GURU

Sikhs believe that they need the guidance of a Guru to reach God. The term is derived from a Sanskrit word meaning 'heavy': hence a Guru is a teacher of 'heavy' or 'weighty' matters. The Guru leads the soul from darkness to light.

THE SPARK

Nanak followed Hinduism more by affirming that there is a divine spark within each person, as in the concept of the *atman*. This states that the deepest level of the human soul is in fact divine, and a part of God that needs to return to him. The soul can respond to God's word through the Guru and through chanting the name of God. This is an awakening and a calling forth.

THE *GURBANI*

The term *gurbani* means 'utterance(s) of the Guru'. Nanak's teaching can be summed up in four points:

❋ There is one God both within and beyond this world.

❋ The cycle of rebirth exists, and people must pass through this until they are purified.

❋ The goal of each person is to rejoin with God – *mukti*.

❋ Sikhs need to chant, worship and serve others.

The Ek Aum-Kar symbol, which signifies the oneness and unity of God.

Teachers of the Way

'When a lamp is lit, darkness is dispelled. Likewise, by reading spiritual books, the darkness of the mind is destroyed.'

Guru Granth Sahib

THE TEN GURUS

Ten Gurus taught Sikhs that what they believe is an unbroken line of revelation and divine instruction.

Guru Angad (1539–52) Nanak's faithful follower Lehna became the second Guru, appointed by Nanak himself. He took the name Angad. He was instrumental in developing a special language for the Sikhs to write their Scriptures in, Gurmukhi, to give the community a distinctive identity. Angad composed many hymns that were included in the *Guru Granth Sahib*.

Guru Amar Das (1552–74) Amar Das developed the open kitchen, *langar*, as a regular part of Sikh life and worship, so that anyone could sit with him whether in discussion or worship. The Sikh community firmly resisted the Hindu caste restrictions. Each place of worship, *gurdwara*, would then have a *langar*.

Guru Ram Das (1574–81) Ram Das, the fourth Guru, founded the holy city of Amritsar and wrote the hymn that is used to perform Sikh weddings. Up to this time, Sikh couples had to go through Hindu ceremonies to be married.

The return

The soul wanders from birth to birth in its ignorance until it is ready to join with God. Nanak embraced the idea of reincarnation and the constant round of rebirths, *samsara*. The goal is to seek a release or union, which is known as *mukti*. It is similar to the Hindu *moksha* or the Buddhist *nirvana*. The soul needs to be purified by a cluster of devotions and disciplines:

♦ chanting the *Nam*
♦ meditating upon the *Nam*
♦ listening to the teachings of the Gurus, the *gurbani*
♦ worship
♦ acts of service and charity.

It is debatable how Nanak envisaged the return. He spoke of the soul being reabsorbed into God as in the Hindu idea of a raindrop rejoining the ocean, but how personal or self-aware he thought this process was is unclear. It is something transcendent.

Guru Arjan Dev (1581–1606) Arjan, the fifth Guru, was the youngest son of Ram Das. He built a temple, the Harimandir, in the middle of a lake (known as 'the Tank' as it was artificial) in Amritsar. This was later named the Golden Temple. Disciples collected contributions for this on the first day of *Baiksakhi* each year.

Arjan also composed hymns, and he collected the hymns of the other Gurus together and published them as 'the first book', the *Adi Granth*, which later became part of the full collection in the *Guru Granth Sahib*.

Arjan also led charitable projects, opening a leprosy centre.

Arjan was later martyred when the Emperor Jehangir persecuted the Sikhs. He died a horrible death, being roasted alive, and his body was thrown into the river.

Guru Har Gobind (1606–44) Har Gobind carried two swords for warfare and for the truth of the spirit. For Sikhism, this was the beginning of using violence in self-defence. He trained the Sikhs to fight and built a fort at Amritsar. His forces had to withdraw to the mountains on one occasion, and he was captured and imprisoned. His release is celebrated at *Divali*.

Guru Har Rai (1644–61) Har Rai was the grandson of Har Gobind. More persecution struck the Sikh community during this time and they had to withdraw further into the mountains.

Guru Har Krishan (1626–64) Har Krishan, the second son of Har Rai, was only five years old when he became Guru. He set up charitable works to look after smallpox sufferers. He caught the disease and died, the only one of the Gurus who did not marry and have a family.

Guru Tegh Bahadur (1621–75) Tegh Bahadur fought as a warrior against the emperor, who persecuted anyone who

The Mool Mantra.

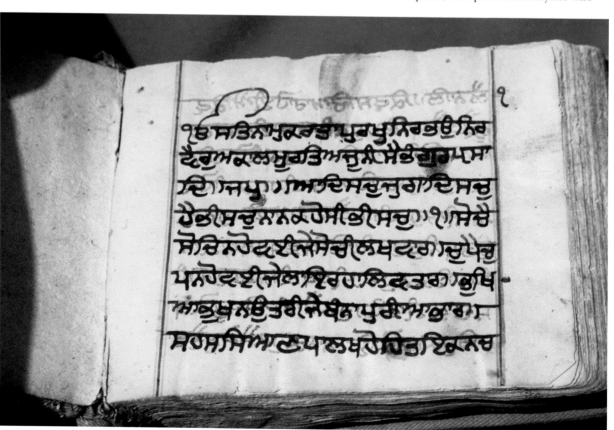

The *Guru Granth Sahib*

All copies of the *Guru Granth Sahib* are written in the Gurmukhi script. The original hymns were written in Punjabi, Hindi, Persian and Sanskrit. There are 1,430 pages and 3,384 hymns. There is also an introduction containing the set prayers for morning, evening and night. The main collection ends with hymns by Hindus and Muslims. Finally there is a collection of short hymns in the form of couplets.

The *Granth* is treated with immense respect. It is carried into the *gurdwara* wrapped in clean linen, on someone's head. The *Granth* always has to be above anyone else. All sit below it and if it is moved, all stand. It is fanned during the services and it is carried away to a side room afterwards where it is laid to rest.

did not agree with his views. The emperor tried to convert Hindu Brahmins, but they turned to Tegh Bahadur for protection. Eventually he was captured, but he refused to convert to Islam. He was then beheaded and became the second martyred Guru.

Guru Gobind Singh (1675–1708) The tenth Guru instituted the *Khalsa* brotherhood and the *Amrit* ceremony. He declared that there would be no more living Gurus. Instead, the book would be the Guru. Gobind Singh collected the various hymns and created the sections of the *Guru Granth Sahib*, giving it its final form with 31 divisions, each beginning with the *Mool Mantra*. He added a hymn of his own and some of Guru Tegh Bahadur's hymns. Thus the *Adi Granth* became 'the revered teacher book', the *Guru Granth Sahib*.

Treasury of the Heart

'There is One God
Whose Name is Truth.
God is the Creator,
And is without fear and
    without hate.
God is timeless,
God's Spirit is throughout
    the universe.
God is not born,
Nor will die to be born again,
God is self-existent.
By the grace of the Gurus God
    is made known to mankind.'

The *Mool Mantra*

THE *MOOL MANTRA*

Sikh belief can be summed up in the *Mool Mantra*, written by Guru Nanak. This stresses that God is without shape or form and must not be imagined: God is self-existent. Nanak teaches God's eternity and covers the age-old question 'Who made God?' If God is God, then nothing can make him. God is Holy Being itself.

The *Mantra* also teaches the grace of God; God teaches humanity through his word spoken through the Gurus. Sikhism, like most faiths, teaches salvation by works up to a point but adds that the mercy and help of God are also needed to raise the soul back to union with the divine. There is a sense of parallel with Islam here, for Allah sent his word down to humanity through his prophets.

The *Mool Mantra* is at the beginning of the *Japji Sahib*, the morning prayer recited by Sikhs. The *Japji* is the opening section of the *Granth* and the collected sayings and hymns of Nanak.

'The *Guru Granth Sahib* is treated with respect like a living Guru. It is always given the place of honour, above everyone else.'

Jasminder, a Sikh teenager from Birmingham, England

✳

The *Mantra* suggests that humans are reincarnated through the cycle of *samsara*, but God is beyond this; the goal of union with him leads to a long purification and many lifetimes. Some Sikh traditions suggest that what you speak out as you are dying reveals your innermost heart and your attachments. If, for example, you speak of your mother, then you will be reborn as a prostitute, as you reveal that you are attached to the flesh and to procreation. Reciting the name of God at death shows a soul that is purified.

TRUTH

The search for truth is a sacred duty for the Sikh. Nanak taught that truth must be sought in the heart, and the truth of God must be found by each person in their own right. Sikhs are taught to recognize the truth of God behind all religions and to respect all faiths, though they have their own distinctive beliefs and customs. The search for truth extends to everyday life and to integrity and honesty in relationships and financial dealings. The search for truth also spurs young people on to work hard at their education.

THE KHALSA

This special brotherhood was set up in 1699 when the tenth Guru, Guru Gobind Singh, called the community together in April, during the New Year festival of *Baisakhi*. He took out his sword, and brandishing this he called out to see if any were willing to die for his faith. One man stepped forward, and the Guru led him into his tent. The Guru came out carrying a bloodstained sword. He called out the challenge again, and four others

Equality

There are no priests in Sikhism, as each person has access to the divine through the *atman* within and through the word of the Gurus. There are specially trained leaders of the Sikh community who can read the Scriptures in the original Gurmukhi script, which was devised for the Sikhs alone to give them a distinctive, cultural identity.

This radical equality extends to the roles of men and women before God. They are equally precious to him. Both sexes can join the *Khalsa*, the special, initiated Sikh brotherhood.

Nanak rejected the Hindu caste system as Buddha had centuries earlier; each soul was open to God and invited to purify itself regardless of birth or status.

followed, one by one. Each time, the Guru held aloft a bloodstained sword. It was a dramatic gesture, a trick to shake the complacency of the community and to test the courage of his followers. Animal's blood had drenched the sword in the tent. The five men were initiated into the *Khalsa* ('the pure ones') by using *amrit*. This is sugar and water in equal proportions mixed in an iron bowl with a two-edged sword called a *khanda*. The worshipper drinks the *amrit* and some is sprinkled upon their hair. Finally, after admitting the five men (known in Sikh lore as 'the Five Faithful Ones', the *panj pyares*) they admitted the Guru. He had been named Guru Gobind Rai, but then he changed his last name to 'Singh' meaning 'Lion'. Thereafter, all Sikh men who joined the *Khalsa* became 'Singh'. Women take the name 'Kaur', 'Princess'.

The establishment of the *Khalsa* was meant to set up a crack force of devotees who would guard the faith, teach it uncompromisingly and fight in self-defence. The *Khalsa* gradually became widened to embrace all adult Sikhs who would devote themselves to greater commitment and obedience to customs and special dress.

Paths to Peace

'Turn to God in contemplation. In calling God to mind find peace. Thus our inner troubles are stilled, and all anguish is driven away.'

Sukhmani Prayer,
Guru Granth Sahib

THE NAME OF GOD

Sikhs are encouraged to chant the name of God, the *Nam*, daily. Prayer beads might be used to help them do this. Sikhs also meditate upon the *Nam*, seeking to draw blessings into themselves.

Sikhism teaches that each individual can find God within without a priest. Not everyone can be a Guru, but they can be 'filled with God' as they meditate upon his name and chant his praises. Despite this, Sikhism does not seem to have developed a mystical streak or mystical teaching (unlike Islam and Hinduism), even though its founder claimed a direct experience of God.

Sikh 'baptism', the amrit ceremony.

DAILY PRAYER

The *Nit nem* is the 'daily rule' of prayer, using set prayers in the morning, evening and at night. Many Sikh homes have a complete copy of the *Guru Granth Sahib,* which is kept on a high shelf above everything else. There are also smaller books that contain extracts from the hymns of the *Gurus.* A selection like this is called the *Gutka.* These can be used like personal prayer books.

The three times of prayer involve reciting the *Japji* hymns, the *Rehiras* and the *Sohilla.* At the end of each of these prayer times Sikhs recite the *Ardas,* which asks for forgiveness and blessing.

HUKAM

Hukam means an order, and when this is applied to a certain method of reading the Scriptures, it means a divine order to follow. The *Granth* is opened at random, and the finger is placed on a passage. This is read as a form of guidance for the moment. This can be done at home, in private or with the family, or in the *gurdwara.*

SEVA

Sikhs are given a strong ethical code in their upbringing and when they join the *Khalsa.* Service or *seva* can take three forms: intellectual, manual or material. Intellectual service involves learning about the faith and explaining it to others; manual is cooking for the needy or serving in the *langar*; material is charitable works.

RAHIT

Rahit means conduct or discipline. There has been a code of conduct since Guru Gobind Singh, but there have been disputes about what was authentic to his teaching. It was only in 1945 that an agreed code, a *Rahit*, was published, having been worked on by the SGPC – the Shiromani Gurdwara Parbandhak Committee, a group responsible for all Sikh places of worship in the Punjab. This has been translated into many languages for Sikhs living abroad. There are moral commandments against stealing, urging Sikhs to earn an honest

The Golden Temple at Amritsar.

Maharaja Ranjit Singh

After the death of Guru Gobind Singh, persecution continued until the emperor's rule grew weaker. Various resistance groups were set up among the Sikhs who were often fighting for their lives. Ranjit Singh became their overall leader in 1792. He united the factions and became the supreme military leader, or *maharaja*. He improved the Harimandir at Amritsar by installing the golden roof and the silver gate, among other things. Other *gurdwaras* were repaired. His rule was peaceful, and he made sure that he included Hindus and Muslims in his army to show respect and toleration. At his court, besides Hindus and Muslims, he even employed foreigners such as Britons and Americans. He died in 1839 and is remembered as a just and fair ruler who lived by the principles of conduct laid down by the Gurus.

Bhagat Puran Singh

Bhagat Puran Singh is a well-known and respected holy man of the twentieth century. Bhagat had come from a poor family, and he worked hard for those who were underprivileged. At the age of 19 he made a vow to be celibate in order to devote his life to the poor. He spent time sweeping the streets and clearing them of rubble and he ensured that any who died with no family were properly cremated. He found an abandoned, disabled child at a *gurdwara* in 1934. He carried him around on his back for years, going about his duties.

In 1947 he founded a Home for the Handicapped, the Pingalwara. He began with a few tents and later acquired buildings. He was nominated for the Nobel Peace Prize in 1991 and was known as the 'Mother Teresa of Punjab'.

Bhagat Puran Singh 'had nothing except his single-minded dedication to serve the poor and needy. And yet he was able to help thousands of lepers, mentally and physically handicapped, and the dying.'

Khushwant Singh, a Sikh writer

'There can be no love of God without active service.'

Japji Prayer, **Guru Granth Sahib**

❋

living, as well as encouraging voluntary service. Sikhs are asked to avoid intoxicating substances, and women should not pierce the nose or ears. Neither is it proper for a Sikh woman to wear a veil and hide her face – she is equal to a man and it is her glory.

Awe and Wonder

'Sing God's praise, hear it sung, and let your heart be filled with love. God will bring peace to your home and take away all your sadness.'

Guru Granth Sahib

THE *GURDWARA*

Dwara means 'door' or 'gate'; *gurdwara* means 'door of the Guru'. People assemble in the *gurdwara* to hear the *gurbani*. A *gurdwara* is any building for public worship that has a complete copy of the *Guru Granth Sahib* inside.

Gurdwaras can be of many different designs, but they will all have a saffron flag flying outside. This shows the *Khanda*, the symbol of the *Khalsa* with the double-edged sword, the two swords of battle and the spirit, and a circle denoting the one God. The flag is called the *Nishan Sahib*. Sikhs take the saffron colour from Indian culture as this is the colour of the rising sun and thus of life and purity.

INSIDE THE *GURDWARA*

Worshippers remove their shoes in the outer hall of the *gurdwara* as a sign of respect, and both men and women cover their heads. People are expected not to take tobacco or alcohol inside.

The worship hall will be plain with little decoration. There might be coloured lights or tinsel streamers. Besides these there will be some pictures of the Gurus. These are only used as visual aids or decoration, and there are no devotional practices attached to them. They are not worshipped.

The focal point for the worshippers is a stand called a *palki*. In the centre of this is a raised platform called a *manji* where the *Guru Granth Sahib* rests. When it is not being read it is covered with a colourful, embroidered cloth called a *romala*.

The *Granth*

A *granthi* is trained to read the Gurmukhi language of the *Guru Granth Sahib*, and he sits behind it, just beneath it. A fan made of hair, a *chauri*, is waved over the book continually by the *granthi* or an attendant. The *chauri* has its origins in cooling and keeping insects at bay in a hot country, but it is also a symbol of authority.

The *Granth* is laid to rest at the end of the day. The Scriptures are wrapped in a clean *romala* and another cloth is placed on the *granthi's* head. He carries the book on his head, so that it is always held in the highest place, as another Sikh walks behind with the *chauri*. The *Granth* is taken to a special room, high up in the building, and laid to rest until the morning. It is covered by more *romalas*.

Above the *palki* is a canopy, a *chandi*. The area where the *Granth* rests is called a throne, a *takht*.

Besides the worship room and the room where the *Granth* is laid to rest, there will be schoolrooms, maybe a library, possibly private accommodation for the *granthi*, and the dining room, the *langar*.

WORSHIP

Sikhs do not have a set day throughout all their communities for the act of worship, or *diwan*. This tends to fit in with the holy days of their host nation. In the UK and the USA it is a Sunday.

On entering the worship hall worshippers approach the *takht*, then bow low and present an offering. If this is money it will be put in a special box. Offerings of food and drink might also be made.

There are no seats. Everyone sits cross-legged on the floor. It is a mark of disrespect to sit with your feet pointing towards the *Granth*. Men and women tend to sit on different sides of the hall, though they are not instructed to. Seated thus they form the community, the *sangat* (from a similar word to the Buddhist *sangha*).

The worship session consists of *kirtan*, singing hymns from the *Granth*. These are led by musicians, *ragis*, with drums and a harmonium. The hymns may be explained before they are sung, and there might be section of teaching from the *Granth*. During the *kirtan*, people might meditate upon the names of God, some using prayer beads.

The *langar*

The *langar* was established as a communal dining room at every *gurdwara* by Guru Amar Das. Guru Nanak had encouraged people to eat together with him when they travelled to listen to him. He had reinforced the message that all were equal before God and the caste system was to be rejected. Later, all Sikh worship concluded with a shared meal. Any visitors are welcome. This will be a vegetarian meal so that no one is offended (although Sikhs do not have to be vegetarians).

All members of the community will take their turn preparing the meal on a rota system, including the richer, professional members. This teaches them the value of performing service, *seva*.

At the closing part of the worship, special food is shared among all present, the *karah prashad*. This is a sweet paste made of equal parts of sugar, butter, water and semolina. Before it is shared out, part of the *Japji* is recited and after closing prayers, all stand to face the *Granth* while a prayer is said over the *karah prashad* as it is touched with a ceremonial sword, a *kirpan*.

Anyone, Sikh or non-Sikh, is welcome to share this food. Only a small portion is given out to each person as it is just a token.

Journey into Mystery

'God has sent this wonderful gift; conceived by grace may he live many years.'

Guru Arjan

THE MYSTERY OF GOD

Ek Aum-kar, 'God is One', is a central Sikh belief. God is transcendent, holy, beyond understanding, and yet condescends to teach the Gurus, and those who commune with their spirits. Through the *gurbani* and the teachings of the *Granth*, Sikhs can draw close to God and contemplate his word. The divine names can be recited, and phrases such as *Waheiguru*, 'Wonderful Lord' are repeated throughout worship to invoke the presence of God.

God is mysterious and vast, but also close to the human heart.

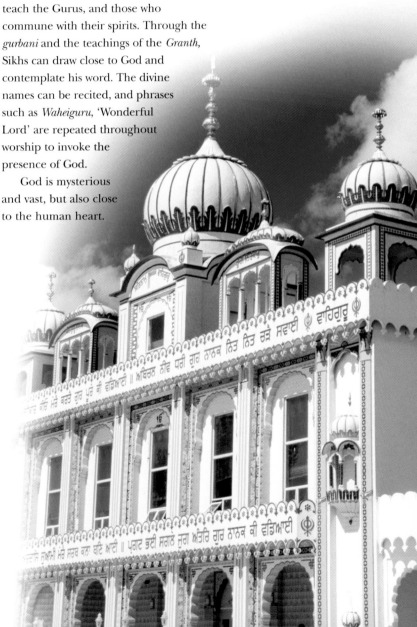

The Golden Temple.

THE MYSTERY OF THE GURUS

There is a mystery about how the Gurus believed that God spoke to them, and why they were specially chosen to hear his voice. There is a mystery about the calling of Guru Nanak, his summons to the Court of Heaven. He recorded little about it and we do not know exactly what happened to him. A mystery also surrounds his death in Sikh tradition. When he was on his deathbed, his followers argued about what to do with his body. Should it be cremated or buried? Nanak asked them to leave two bunches of flowers, one on either side of him. Whichever did not wither by the morning showed the right course of action. In the morning, his body had gone and both bunches were blossoming.

Joyful celebrations at a gurpurb.

BIRTH

The birth of a child is considered a great blessing from God by Sikhs. The child is taken to the *gurdwara* and the *Granth* is opened at random to perform a *hukam*. The hymn on that page is read, and the child's name must begin with the first letter of that hymn.

AMRITSANKAR

Amritsankar is the initiation ceremony that might mark a coming of age, but this can be delayed until well into adulthood. Candidates assemble and are asked a number of searching questions:

❁ Are they willing to learn and to follow Sikh teachings?
❁ Will they pray to only one God?
❁ Will they serve humanity?

A *hukam* is read from the *Granth*, and then the *amrit* is prepared. Sugar and water, in equal proportions, are mixed with a double-edged sword in an iron bowl by five men representing 'the five faithful ones', the *panj pyare*. Each candidate kneels and drinks a handful of *amrit*, saying each time: *Waheiguru ji Khalsa, Waheiguru ji Fateh*. ('The *Khalsa* is dedicated to God. The victory belongs to God.')

The Five Ks

There are five things that Sikhs who are admitted into the *Khalsa* must agree to wear. These are the *Panj Kakke*:

1. *Kesh* – uncut hair kept clean as a sign of devotion to God. This is covered by the turban.
2. *Kangha* – a comb that keeps the hair tidy and clean and that helps to tie it up.
3. *Kara* – a steel bracelet worn around the right wrist. The circle reminds them of the One God who is eternal and also of the unity of the Khalsa.
4. *Kachha* – loose shorts worn as an undergarment. These might have been introduced to enable ease of running and fighting.
5. Kirpan – a short sword. This is a reminder of the duty to protect the weak.

DEATH

For a Sikh, death is a release into the path of God, into his mercy and into the hands of *karma*. How one has lived determines what will happen, and Sikhs believe in reincarnation, taking this from Hinduism. The *Granth* will be read beside the bedside of a dying person, and the *Granth* will be turned to for comfort by the bereaved. Through the word of God, and through the purification of the soul, release will be found from the cycle of rebirth, *samsara*. A hymn often sung at Sikh funerals puts it this way:

> *'The dawn of a new day is the herald of a sunset.*
> *Earth is not our permanent home.*
> *Life is like a shadow on the wall.'*

'When all other means to curb tyranny fail, it is lawful to take up the sword.'
Guru Gobind Singh

'I carry the *kirpan* to remind me of my duty to help the weak. If someone is attacked by muggers or thugs, I should spring to their defence.'
Sikh youth from Slough, England

'Each day that dawns must reach its end; all must leave for none may stay. Our friends take their leave, we must also go. Death is our fate, our journey long.'
Guru Granth Sahib

Amritsar

Amritsar means 'pool of nectar' and the city was built upon land bought by Guru Ram Das. It was also known as Ramdaspur, for Guru Ram Das began building there in 1573. He began the conversion of a natural pool into a manmade lake, 'the Tank', where Sikhs could ritually bathe. The next Guru, Arjan Dev, continued the building and developed the Tank. He had the Harimandir built in the centre, the Golden Temple, which was later adorned with sheets of gold and marble ornamentation. The temple was completed in 1601, and the *Adi Granth* was placed there soon after.

The Golden Temple has two storeys with a throne, *takht*, below which *ragis* sing hymns continually. Upstairs there is a constant reading of the Granth in its entirety. A hall of mirrors surrounds the worshippers, a decoration that was only used by emperors at the time. This marks the area as sacred. The temple is crowned by a golden dome. The Golden Temple is also known as *Darbar Sahib*, 'the Court of the Lord'. One enters it by stepping down to denote humility, and there are doors on all four sides to show that Sikhism is open to all.

Guru Nanak did not encourage ideas of pilgrimage, teaching that God was to be found everywhere. In one sense there is nothing special about the Golden Temple as God can be worshipped in any *gurdwara*, but it is a heritage, a precious centre of worship for Sikhs, which also contains a museum showing many artefacts from Sikh history.

Making Merry

'Victory to the True Lord!'

Sikh chant

GURPURBS

Purb means 'day' and a *gurpurb* celebrates something in the life of one of the Gurus. There are four main *gurpurbs*. Two celebrate the births of Guru Nanak and Guru Gobind Singh and two commemorate the martyrdoms of Guru Arjan and Guru Tegh Bahadur. Hymns composed by the particular Guru will be sung in the *gurdwara*. There will often be a procession of the *Granth* through the streets. A *takht*, and a *palki*, are set up on the back of a lorry and driven along. Five Sikh men dress ceremonially and walk in front, representing the 'five faithful ones', the *panj pyare*.

The whole of the *Granth* will be read through, taking 48 hours and a team of readers. This begins two days before the *gurpurb* and is called an *Akhand Path*. *Karah prashad* is provided and shared out for those present during the reading.

The martyrdoms of Guru Arjan and Guru Tegh Bahadur are also celebrated in the *gurdwaras* and their hymns are sung. Sikhism cherishes its martyr gurus, as the people have gone through many times of persecution and suffering. The tenth Guru, Gobind Singh, succeeded the martyred Guru Tegh Bahadur. Two of his sons, Baba Zorawar Singh and Baba Fateh Singh, were captured and put to death. His determination to defend the Sikhs and to form the *Khalsa* can thus be understood, as well as his inspiration to make the *Granth* the Guru of the people, thus avoiding any dynastic rivalry and attempts on the lives of future leaders.

BAISAKHI

Baisakhi is the main Sikh spring festival, the New Year in April. It recalls the formation of the *Khalsa* when Guru Gobind Singh called the Sikhs together. This is the traditional time for initiation, the *Amritsankar*. At this time, the flag and pole (the *Nishan Sahib*) are taken down from the *gurdwara*. The old flag is torn up and people take a portion home to treasure. The pole is cleansed with yoghurt and water and then the new flag is attached and raised up.

DIVALI

Sikhs celebrate this Hindu festival, but they invest it with their own content.

Candles and lamps are lit to remember the release from prison of Guru Har Gobind. Apparently, he refused to go unless 52 other prisoners, Hindu princes, were released with him. The emperor granted his request only as long as the 52 clung onto the Guru's cloak. All of them left, clutching the tassels on his cloak.

HOLA MAHALLA

This is a minor holiday that was started by Guru Gobind Singh. The name means 'attack or be attacked'. It was a festival for military training and exercises, and there are mock battles today in the Punjab. Sikhs compete in archery and wrestling competitions.

Military training at the festival of Hola Mahalla.

Today

'Your teaching is true, your word is sweet, your eyes see everything, you are calmness itself.'

Guru Granth Sahib

KHALISTAN AND THE PUNJAB

Sikhs have struggled for freedom to worship as they please many times in the history of their faith. When India was part of the British empire, Sikhs had no control over their own *gurdwaras.* In 1919, a massacre took place at Amritsar when many Sikhs gathered to celebrate *Baisakhi.* They did not have permission for the gathering, and though it was

The Sikh leader Jarnail Singh Bhindranwale speaking outside the Golden Temple.

peaceful, with many women and children present, British troops assembled and opened fire, killing many. This event shocked India and led to vociferous Sikh protests. An Act of Parliament in 1925 gave Sikhs control of their places of worship.

In 1947, India obtained independence. A separate Muslim state was set up – Pakistan. The Sikhs campaigned for their own homeland in the Punjab, to be called Khalistan. They were ignored, and many were made homeless by the new national frontiers.

Campaigns wax and wane, and violence has broken out from time to time in India since. In 1984, the Indian army damaged Amritsar causing

widespread shock. The Indian Prime Minister, Indira Gandhi, was assassinated by her two Sikh bodyguards, and the action of these two men caused the whole community to feel scapegoated for a time. This has stirred up many young Sikhs who were becoming indifferent about their faith and its traditions. To make matters worse, a Sikh leader, Saint Jarnail Singh Bhindranwale, a hero to the youth, was killed in the attack on Amritsar in 1984.

WOMEN

The role of women in the Sikh community is radical and strong. The Gurus sought to introduce equality. Guru Nanak said, 'Why should we call her inferior, who gives birth to great men?' A Sikh woman can take any role that a Sikh man can in their community and worship. Child brides were banned in the time of the Gurus, as was *sati*, the custom of widows throwing themselves on the funeral pyres of their husbands.

BOLLYWOOD

The Indian film industry, 'Bollywood', relies heavily on Punjabi citizens. Sikhs are influential in this industry. Although many Bollywood films are love stories about marriage and courtship, recent projects have involved the lives of freedom fighters such as Shaheed Udham Singh, who was present at Amritsar during the massacre by the British in 1919. In 1940, he assassinated the former governor of the Punjab in London. Shaheed was arrested and executed for his crime, and his ashes were taken back to India in 1975.

White Sikhs

The *Gora*, or White Sikh, phenomenon, began in the USA in the 1970s with the 3HO movement ('Healthy, Happy, Holy Organisation') started by Harbhajan Singh Puri, also known as Yogi Bhaajan. White converts follow a strict, traditional Sikh code, adhering to the *Rahit Maryada* published in the Punjab in the 1950s. Their existence was unexpected as the Sikh movement was local to the Punjab and a very Indian affair. The *Gora* have highlighted tensions within the Sikh community. For example, though Sikhism rejects the caste system, in practice, many Sikhs are conscious of belonging to one of the social castes of Indian society, and these can help to determine marriage arrangements and the ownership of certain *gurdwaras*. The *Gora* do not fit into any pattern of caste, and they can have difficulty being totally accepted into the wider Sikh community.

Another tension is shown up between three main groups, the *Amritdhari*, the *Kesdhari* and the *Sahajdhari*. The *Amritdhari* have undergone the *Amrit Sankar* ceremony and wear the Five Ks. The *Kesdhari* wear the Five Ks but have not taken the vows of the *Amrit Sankar* ceremony. The *Sahajdhari* do not wear the Five Ks and they cut their hair. They are more Western in style. The *Gora* denounce those who cut their hair as not being true Sikhs. Indeed, Westernization among the younger generation away from the Punjab is a major concern for Sikh communities.

The Sikh pop group, Cornershop.

MUSIC

Bhangra is a traditional form of music and dance performed at harvest time using traditional Indian drums (*dhol, dholak* and *tabla*). *Bhangra* music today has entered the pop charts in India and in the West. Some groups, such as Alaap, whose lead singer is Channi Singh, use Western instruments as well.

Some, such as the performer Apache Indian, combine reggae or rap with the traditional rhythms. A popular DJ from a Punjabi background is Bally Sagoo. The UK has seen groups such as Safri Boyz from Birmingham and Cornershop from Preston. The latter is named after the popular stereotype of the Asian family running the local corner shop.

SIKHISM	at a glance...

- ♦ When did it begin? – in fifteenth century CE India.
- ♦ The founder – Guru Nanak (1469–1539 CE) who sought to unite Muslims and Hindus in a synthesis of their main beliefs. Nine other Gurus succeeded him, who developed the faith further.
- ♦ God – There is one God who alone is worshipped.
- ♦ Redeemer figure – The Gurus are only teachers, but they are chosen by the grace of God who delights to use them to teach people. Freedom from rebirth is sought by service, good deeds and worship.
- ♦ Scriptures – The *Guru Granth Sahib* is a collection of many hymns from the different gurus. This is treated as the final and living Guru for all ages.

- ♦ Beliefs – There is one God who sends his Gurus. The caste system is rejected and all are equal before God. Sikhs have a duty to become initiated and to wear symbols of their faith, the Five Ks.
- ♦ Place of worship – The *gurdwara*, 'the gate of the Guru'. A copy of the *Granth* is kept inside, and people sit in the prayer hall.
- ♦ Sacred food – Sikhs share food to emphasize their equality. In the worship service, they share *prashad*. Afterwards, in the *langar*, they eat a meal together.
- ♦ Main festivals – *Baisakhi* is the New Year festival. *Divali* is the festival of light. *Gurpurbs* celebrate the lives of the ten Gurus.
- ♦ Key symbols – the circle with the three swords; their flag, the *Nishan Sahib*. The *Ek Aum-kar* phrase remembers that there is one God.

'I have immense faith… in God. It's with His help I've got where I am today. Being a Sikh, I pray every morning and, especially, before going on stage to do a show.'
Malkit Singh, *Bhangra* singer

'Hearing of the troubles in the Punjab made me wake up to my calling as a Sikh. I had not been bothering about our customs, but I realized that I was under attack, too. I now wear the turban and the Five Ks.'
Arjan, a Sikh young man from London, England

✳

Judaism

'My father was a wandering Aramean and he went down into Egypt with a few people, and lived there and became a great nation...'

Deuteronomy 26:5

The Jewish faith goes back to about 2,000 BCE and the early beliefs and hopes of Semitic peoples in the Near East. Desert nomads gave way to settled communities as a group of tribes was bound by a covenant, a spiritual agreement to serve God and to aid one another. These tribes gave humanity the Law of Moses, the teachings of the prophets and the hope of a Messiah.

THE LAND

The stories of the ancestors trace their roots to what is now known as Israel, but was then the land of Canaan. The tribes occupied the hill country of Judea and eventually made Jerusalem their capital city. A series of monarchs united them in later years, the most famous of whom was David. They gradually took control of the surrounding territory and the coastal plain.

WANDERERS

The early name for the tribes was 'the Hebrews', a term that means something like traveller or wanderer. It means, literally, 'from the other side', in other words, from across the River Tigris and the River Euphrates. The stories of the ancestors have them journeying to Canaan from the Gulf area. 'Hebrew' might be the same as a term in ancient texts, *Habiru*, who were unsettled groups of people. Their ancestors are sometimes called 'Arameans'. Early in the cycle of ancestor sagas, the name Israel is introduced. This was the new name given to the ancestor Jacob after a revelation of God. The Hebrews became the Israelites, and later, the term 'Jew' meant someone from the land of Judea. This was the southern part of the kingdom that remained after the north had been conquered by Assyrians. So, Hebrew, Israelite, Jew: three names but one race. Over the years, different types of Judaism have emerged. From the time of the Temple there were priests and sacrifices, then local rabbis and synagogues after the fall of Jerusalem in 70 CE. The rabbis were specially trained in the Law, the *Torah*, and the oral traditions of their people, the *Halakhah*.

FAMOUS JEWS

Jews have made contributions to history, particularly in the West. Karl Marx, for example, helped found Communism. Sigmund Freud developed psychoanalysis and counselling. Jonas Salk discovered the polio vaccine. Stephen Spielberg is a film director and Barbara Streisand is a famous Hollywood actress.

In a nutshell

Judaism believes in election by God. Their race was chosen, called, by the one God to learn his laws and represent his ways to the nations. They were bound to God by the covenant with Moses, their greatest leader and prophet. A covenant is a solemn promise, a binding oath between two parties. The people were given the Law to follow to keep their part of the bargain; God set their ancestors free from slavery in Egypt and they followed him out of gratitude.

The responsibility of this calling became clear with the passing of time. They were to be 'a light to the nations' and God's purposes were frustrated if the people abandoned his laws.

The genius

Judaism has a God who binds himself to his people and they serve him freely and joyfully. They are honoured to be his chosen people. He promises never to desert them and to see his purposes worked out in history.

The symbol

The hexagram, or six-pointed star of David, was based upon a common symbol and charm in the ancient Near East. This was used by Jews, Christians

'To be a Jew is to belong, to belong to an ancient people and to own customs and traditions that guide you through life. It is a great privilege.'
Jonathan, a Jewish father

✳

The psychoanalyst Sigmund Freud.

and Muslims alike for a time, and it only became the symbol of the Jewish faith as late as the nineteenth century. Earlier, Jewish mystics had used it, with names of God written in Hebrew inscribed around the two interlocking triangles. This made it spiritually powerful, hence the name *Magen David*, 'Star of David'.

First Steps

'In the beginning God created the heavens and the earth. Now, the earth was formless and empty, darkness was over the surface of the deep, and the Spirit of God was hovering over the waters.'

Genesis 1:1–2

CREATION

The Hebrew Bible begins with the story of creation. In a great sweeping narrative, the cosmos and the ecosystem are established in seven days or periods of time. In the second chapter of the first book, *Bereshit* in Hebrew, or Genesis in English translations, the first man and woman are featured. Adam is the name of the man, a generic name meaning 'humanity' and 'red', echoing the red clay from which he came. Woman, Eve, meaning 'mother of the living', is made from his side. This beautiful story shows that men and women are of one substance and co-equal. By contrast, in many parts of the Near East when this was written, women were definitely the inferior sex and the possessions of their husbands.

Jews debate the historicity of these stories. Many Orthodox Jews take them as literal fact, as conservative Christians do. Others see them as parables, as wonderful insights into humanity's relationship with God.

Adam and Eve are expelled from Eden after they disobey God and eat from the forbidden tree. If this story is symbolic, then the tree's fruit stands for 'doing your own thing', for self-

Adam and Eve are expelled from the Garden of Eden.

fulfilment. In the ancient world, 'good and evil' denoted the totality of experience, so 'knowing good and evil' meant taking your destiny into your own hands. Thus the relationship with the Creator was broken, and chaos broke out in the world. Judaism does not have a doctrine of original sin as in Christianity, but the world is fallen and people are born with a moral weakness, an inclination to evil, the *yetzer hara*.

ABRAHAM

With the story of Abraham we enter locatable and dateable history. He came from Ur in the Gulf area, which was excavated by Sir Leonard Woolley in the early twentieth century. He found the huge *ziggurat* temples to the sun god, for example. Abraham sensed a call from God to leave this land, and he made his way along the rivers to the north, to the land of Haran. From there he entered Canaan where his ancestors dwelt. He travelled from oasis to oasis, herding his cattle and worshipping God at simple, stone altars. He was promised a son and heir, Isaac, and through him, all the nations of the earth would be blessed.

The Abraham saga cannot be dated precisely, though. Semitic groups were wandering in search of pasture and permanent land from about 2000 to 1700 BCE.

THE PROPHETS

According to the book of Deuteronomy, God promised to raise up other prophets after Moses to guide the people. One third of the Hebrew Bible contains the oracles of the prophets. The prophets were mainly forthtellers – explaining the consequences of behaving in a certain

Moses

Moses is the greatest prophet of Judaism. He was brought up as an Egyptian prince, though a Hebrew. His name is probably a shortened form of his Egyptian royal name, such as 'Thutmoses' meaning 'son of Thut'. He would have dropped the reference to a pagan deity after his conversion to the God of the Hebrews. By his time many of the Hebrews were enslaved in Egypt and he led them to freedom. The narrative in the second book of the Hebrew Bible, Exodus, reveals a series of plagues that struck the land, ending with the death of the firstborn sons of the Egyptians. Then the Hebrews escaped across the Sea of Reeds, a marshy lake north of the Red Sea, and gathered at settlements in the wilderness of the Sinai peninsula. They gathered at the sacred Mount Sinai, and Moses went up the mountain, leaving the people camped below. He returned with two stone tablets engraved with the Ten Commandments and taught the people that they were to be bound in service to God by a covenant. These commandments formed the core of the *Torah* – a Hebrew word meaning 'Law', 'Way' or 'Revelation'.

There are debates between Orthodox and Reform Jews about how much of the *Torah* was given to Moses on Sinai. The Orthodox think that all 613 commandments were revealed then; the Reform believe that only the core of the laws was, maybe only the Ten Commandments. Others were added later, and sometimes by leaders later than Moses.

Moses and the name of God

Moses had a vision of a burning bush and felt the call of God to return to Egypt to set the Hebrews free:

> 'Now Moses was tending the flock of Jethro his father-in-law, the priest of Midian, and he led the flock to the far side of the desert and came to Horeb, the mountain of God. There the angel of the Lord appeared to him in flames of fire from within a bush. Moses saw that though the bush was on fire it did not burn up. So Moses thought, "I will go over and see this strange sight – why the bush does not burn up."
>
> When the Lord saw that he had gone over to look, God called to him from within the bush, "Moses! Moses!"
>
> And Moses said, "Here I am."
>
> "Do not come any closer," God said. "Take off your sandals, for the place where you are standing is holy ground." Then he said, "I am the God of your father, the God of Abraham, the God of Isaac and the God of Jacob." At this, Moses hid his face, because he was afraid to look at God.
>
> Moses said to God, Suppose I go to the Israelites and say to them, "The God of your fathers has sent me to you," and they ask me, 'What is his name?' Then what shall I tell them?"
>
> God said to Moses, "I AM WHO I AM. This is what you are to say to the Israelites: 'I AM has sent me to you.'"

Exodus 3:1–6, 13–14

Here, God reveals himself as Yahweh (sometimes written in English as Jehovah). That is the best guess as to how it would have been said, for so sacred is this name to the Jews that it is never pronounced. They substitute the word 'Adonai' ('Lord') whenever it appears in the Hebrew Scriptures. Some Jews today, when writing the word 'God' in English, show their respect for the divine name by omitting the 'o', writing 'G–d'.

Early Hebrew had no written vowels, and all that we know is that YHWH, known as the Tetragrammaton, is the given name. It means something like 'Eternal One', 'He who is', 'I am'. Yahweh is identified with El, the God of Abraham, Isaac and Jacob, in Moses' vision. It is not clear if this name was known earlier. Writing found in ancient Ebla might show the form Yah, but this is disputed.

The book of Genesis suggests that people did call on the name of Yahweh much earlier than Moses:

> 'At that time men began to call on the name of the Lord.'

Genesis 4:26

way – rather than foretellers of future events. They spoke the word of God to their contemporaries. However, there are some future prophecies about coming judgement or the coming of the Messiah. 'Messiah' in Hebrew means 'anointed one' and refers to the practice of anointing a new king with holy oil.

DAVID AND THE KINGDOM

The tribes desired a king to rule over them, and a line of kings was established with David. He had been in the service of the first king, Saul, until he fell from favour and lived as a mercenary during his years of exile. David won the throne and established a dynasty that the prophets declared would last for all time. Sadly, after his reign, the nation split into the northern kingdom of Israel and the southern kingdom of Judea. The northern kingdom was defeated and exiled by the Assyrians in 722–721 BCE. The southern was defeated by Babylon in 586 BCE and many were exiled. The Judeans returned some years later and slowly rebuilt their nation. By the time of Jesus, the kings were ruling by approval of Rome and the people were hoping for a new king who would free them again. This did not happen, and Jerusalem fell in 70 CE after a bloody rebellion. Many Jews scattered and lived in the Roman empire, which later became Europe.

With no temple and no king, there was a crisis of faith, but local gatherings of Jewish men had kept the faith alive through the days of Babylonian exile and beyond. These gatherings, or synagogues, to use the Greek term, became the mainstay of the Jewish faith and still are, apart from the practice of the faith in the home.

The Goal

> *'God said to Moses, "I AM WHO I AM"...'*
>
> Exodus 3:14

FROM EL TO YAHWEH

In the stories of the Hebrew Patriarchs – Abraham, Isaac and Jacob – in the *Torah*, God is often referred to as El or as Elohim. The name El was an ancient Semitic name for God which was widespread in the land of Canaan. Abraham travelled to and fro between sacred sites such as the oaks of Mamre where he called upon El. Sometimes El was given special titles such as El-Elyon ('The Most High') or El-Shaddai ('God Almighty').

Abraham felt called to leave Ur and travel back to the land of his ancestors, Canaan, where he seems to have more of an affinity with the natural religion of

'I am the Lord your God, who brought you out of Egypt, out of the land of slavery...'
Exodus 19:2

'The Lord appeared to Abraham near the great trees of Mamre while he was sitting at the entrance to his tent in the heat of the day.'
Genesis 18:1

✳

Oak trees like these would have formed a sacred grove at the time of Abraham.

that people. He was called by El, and bound to El by a covenant that involved the sacrificing of several animals. In turn, El promised blessings to Abraham and his offspring.

After this, the worship of El receded among the people of Canaan and was largely supplanted by a new fertility cult, that of Ba'al. Later Israelite prophets condemned this worship as idolatry.

Elohim is the plural form of El, meaning 'the Godhead', 'God'.

BELIEF IN ONE GOD BECOMES BELIEF IN THE ONLY GOD

The Patriarchs and Moses worshipped only one God, but they assumed that there were many other deities around. They were bound to the service of one only. This is called monolatry. Many ancients believed that each nation had its gods, or chief god, and that if you

Fire is a symbol for God in the Hebrew Scriptures.

worshipped that deity, you needed to stand on the soil of that nation. It was the later prophets who denounced belief in other gods and embraced a clear, uncompromising belief that only one God really existed. This is called monotheism.

ANGELS, WORD AND SPIRIT, *SHEKINAH*

The Hebrew Scriptures reveal a willingness of God to get involved with his people. Various intermediary figures enable God to do this. Early parts of the Scriptures speak of the 'Angel of the Lord' as a powerful, solitary figure who guides the Hebrews. This figure almost seems like a projection, an extension of God's being, though later ideas clearly saw the angels as a heavenly race who were the servants or messengers of God.

The 'Angel' gave way to the idea of the Word and the Spirit, parallel ideas that expressed the power and presence of God on the earth. In Hebrew thought, a word was not something abstract but the expression of a person's thoughts, a powerful force that affected reality. God's Word was even more powerful, and it was the creative power behind the cosmos. The creation story in Genesis chapter 1 has God speaking the world into being, stage by stage.

The Spirit is the indwelling, guiding presence that gives life to the earth. The Spirit enters creatures to give them life. The Word and the Spirit were extensions of God's power. In Christian thought, they were developed into Persons of the Trinity.

The *Shekinah*, or the Glory, was God's presence, usually symbolized by a cloud or a pillar of fire, that dwelt with his people on earth and guided them.

Names for God

In the *Torah*, there are eight names of God that are compounded with Yahweh:

- Yahweh-tsidkenu (The Lord our Righteousness)
- Yahweh-m'kaddesh (The Lord who Sanctifies)
- Yahweh-shammah (The Lord is There)
- Yahweh-shalom (The Lord is Peace)
- Yahweh-rophe (The Lord is a Healer)
- Yahweh-jireh (The Lord Provides)
- Yahweh-nissi (The Lord is our Banner)
- Yahweh-rohi (The Lord is a Shepherd)

THE VISION OF GOD

The Hebrew Bible contains various stories of divine encounters and visionary experiences. These might happen to the Patriarchs or to prophets such as Isaiah. He had a shattering vision of God's holiness.

Ezekiel had a vision of glory, featuring heavenly creatures and a chariot:

> 'Wherever the spirit would go, they would go, and the wheels would rise along with them, because the spirit of the living creatures was in the wheels'..
>
> Ezekiel 1:20

Prophecy seems to have ended among the Jews about 400 years before Jesus. After the trauma of the destruction of the Temple in 70 CE, some began striving after a vision or experience of God as described in the pages of the Bible. Various forms of Jewish mysticism have flourished through the ages, such as the *Merkavah* who sought to spiritually rise with Ezekiel's chariot and enter heaven, or the *Hekhalot* who sought to enter the palaces of heaven in the Spirit.

Jewish mysticism seeks hidden meanings in the words of the Scriptures and is often closely guarded as a secret that is passed on to a pupil by a rabbi. Unlike mysticism in some other faiths, there is no attempt to unify with the Godhead, but to follow his commandments and to heal creation. The healing of creation involves a balancing within God, for God is hurt by the pain of his universe, and part of him, his *Shekinah*, or Glory, is at work within it, almost in exile from the source of the divine.

Teachers of the Way

> 'Be careful to obey all the law my servant Moses gave you; do not turn from it to the right or to the left, that you may be successful wherever you go.'
>
> Joshua 1:7

THE *TORAH*

The greatest collection of teaching for Jews is the *Torah*. *Torah* comes from the Hebrew word *yorah*, 'to teach'.

This forms the first five books of the Hebrew Bible and contains 613 laws. It also contains many stories of the ancestors, and especially the exodus from Egypt. Jews embrace the obligations of the Law out of gratitude for being chosen. The exodus is the dramatic story of the escape from slavery in Egypt; many ancient peoples would not have

> 'I saw the Lord seated on a throne, high and exalted, and the train of his robe filled the temple.'
>
> Isaiah 6:1

> 'God is the centre, the hope, the peace of the world. God brings order and life out of chaos, and he can do so in our lives, too. Following his *mitzvoth* (commandments) is an act of gratitude and worship for his greatness.'
>
> Rachel, an American Jewess

> 'I am God, and there is no other; I am God and there is none like me. I make known the end from the beginning, from ancient times, what is still to come.'
>
> Isaiah 46:9–10

✳

told such a story of their ancestors. They would have invented a new origin and glossed over the facts. There is humility and honesty in the story of the exodus.

The Hebrew names for the five books are taken from the first words of each book in Hebrew:

✳ Genesis/*Bereshit* – 'Beginning'
✳ Exodus/*Shemot* – 'Names'
✳ Leviticus/*Vayikra* –'And He Called'
✳ Numbers/*Bamidbar* – 'In the Wilderness'
✳ Deuteronomy/*Devarim* – 'Words'

Public reading of the *Torah* dates from the time of Ezra the scribe (c. 444 BCE), and the custom of dividing this into portions (*parashiyot*) was introduced in the synagogues. These portions were read weekly over one year or three years. The *Torah* was never meant to be read but to be chanted as a sacred text. Rabbis (or a layperson, the 'master of the reading', *ba'al koreh*) are trained to do this.

There are different views about the authorship of the *Torah*. Orthodox Jews believe that the whole of it was dictated by God on Mount Sinai; other, more

Nathan the Syrian commander bathes in the waters of the River Jordan, watched by the prophet Elijah.

liberal Jews believe that various traditions were written down by scribes over the years, with a core of material from Moses himself.

THE *TENAKH*

The Hebrew Bible is sometimes called the *Tenakh*, which is an acronymn for the three sections of the *Torah*, the *Nevi'im* and the *Ketuvim* (the Law, the Prophets and the Writings).

The Prophets contain the books of the many prophets, plus the histories of the first tribes and the kings of Israel. These all follow the theme that if the people turn to the Lord they will be blessed. Prophecy seems to have stopped in Judah in the fifth century BCE with the prophet Malachi.

The Hebrew Scriptures were translated into Greek in the third to second centuries BCE. These translations contained some extra books in the canon or list of books, such as Tobit. These books were not included in the Hebrew canon when it was finally agreed in the first century CE.

THE *TALMUD*

When Herod's Temple fell in 70 CE, a *Torah* school was founded at Yavneh, about 25 miles west of Jerusalem. There, rabbis met and ideas flourished until 140 CE, when the academy moved first to Galilee and then to Sepphoris. Rituals and laws were codified and parts of the *Torah* were debated, commentaries were written and the opinions of various rabbis were noted. This group produced a body of teachings and commentaries known as the Palestinian *Talmud*. It was their intention to replace the disbanded Jewish parliament, the Sanhedrin, and

 ### The Writings

The Writings contain proverbs, poems and psalms. The Psalms are a collection of 150 sacred songs and prayers. Some of these would have been used in the Temple worship, and they carry instructions for musicians. Some were by King David or were part of a royal collection. The most famous is Psalm 23, 'The Lord is my Shepherd':

'The Lord is my shepherd,
  I shall not be in want.
He makes me lie down in green pastures,
he leads me beside quiet waters,
  he restores my soul.
He guides me in paths of righteousness
  for his name's sake.
Even though I walk
  through the valley of the shadow
of death, I will fear no evil,
  for you are with me;
your rod and your staff,
  they comfort me.
You prepare a table before me
  in the presence of my enemies.
You anoint my head with oil;
  my cup overflows.
Surely goodness and love will follow me
  all the days of my life,
and I will dwell in the house of the Lord
  for ever.

The Wisdom tradition or school filled the pages with wise sayings such as:

'A gentle answer turns away wrath, but a
  harsh word stirs up anger.'
                              Proverbs 15:1

The Song of Songs is a collection of love poems between the king and his beloved. These are lyrical and erotic. Sexual attraction and intercourse are seen as something to be celebrated between husband and wife as a part of God's good creation.

'The world exists only through the breath of schoolchildren.'
The *Talmud*

When Rabbi Akiba was being tortured to death by the Romans in 135 CE, he said to his pupils, 'All my life I didn't understand what it meant to "say these words with all your heart". Now I understand.'

'The Torah is a light for my feet, a guide through life.'
Jonathan, a Jew from Paris

✳

the Temple, to keep the faith alive. In the Persian empire, rabbis had worked in a similar fashion and produced the Babylonian *Talmud*.

The *Talmud* defines rabbinic Judaism from 70 CE until recent years. The *Talmud* contains the *Mishnah* with its sayings, traditions and commentaries, and the *Gemara*, a collection of further rabbinic commentaries. These works have been both guidance and custom for many Jews through the ages, building upon the *Torah*. Before the *Talmud*, and before 70 CE, Judaism was more fluid and varied, with many emphases and movements such as the Pharisees and Sadducees.

Orthodox Jews studying the Torah.

Treasury of the Heart

'Hear, O Israel: the Lord our God, the Lord is one. Love the Lord your God with all your heart and with all your soul and with all your strength.'

Deuteronomy 6:4–5

THE *SHEMA*

The nearest thing to a Jewish confession of faith is the *Shema. Shema* is the Hebrew word for 'hear', and the *Shema* calls upon Israel to believe in one God only. The full text can be found in Deuteronomy 6:1–25. This commands the Jews to follow the laws of God and to remember

Covenant

The Hebrew Bible presents a number of covenants between God and humanity:

♦ Adam is given dominion over the earth.
♦ Noah is promised that God will never destroy humanity again, the rainbow being the sign of this.
♦ Abraham is promised that his offspring will be many and will bless the nations.
♦ Moses is given the Ten Commandments and a series of sacrifices are instituted to keep the people in covenant relationship.
♦ David's descendants are promised the throne forever.

Covenants were common forms of treaty or binding promise in the ancient Near East. Kings would bind themselves to their people, or to other monarchs. There were promises of protection and blessing, but also clear obligations. If these were not fulfilled, the covenant was broken. Offerings, often involving blood sacrifice, would seal the covenant.

God's covenants gave a promise but were often followed by a transgression and a judgement of some kind. Thus Adam and Eve were expelled from the garden of Eden; Abraham's offspring went into slavery in Egypt; the Israelites worshipped the Golden Calf as Moses came down the mountain; and some of the kings worshipped other gods. There is a pattern of blessing and curse, or rise and fall. The first and second Temples were built and destroyed, and the Jews were scattered throughout the world. Still today they await the coming of the Messiah and the final blessing. The rabbis comment that these stories and covenants remind us of God's dual nature of justice and mercy: in his mercy, God does not rush to bring final judgement upon sin but offers new starts time and time again.

that they were once slaves in Egypt. They are told to teach their children the commandments and to tie them on their hands and foreheads, as well as their doorframes. Thus there are small leather boxes containing small scrolls of Deuteronomy and passages from Exodus that Jewish men wear on their foreheads and on their right hands, and a tiny scroll is fixed to the doors of Jewish homes.

The *Shema* teaches the oneness of Yahweh; no others are to be associated with him, and no other gods should be worshipped or have their names used in oaths.

> *'Shema Yisrael, Adonai Elohenu, Adonai echad…'*
>
> Deuteronomy 6:4

Commitment to one God alone (whether as in monolatry or monotheism) was a radical idea in the ancient world where whole pantheons of gods were worshipped. It was bold and daring. In the days of the Roman empire, Jews were given a special dispensation from worshipping the emperor.

MESSIAH

The term 'Messiah' means 'anointed one' and is synonymous with the king of the Jews. Jewish kings were anointed by the priests with holy oil from a ram's horn. The first king was Saul in the tenth century BCE, followed by David, the greatest of the kings in the Hebrew Bible. He united the tribes and conquered Jerusalem. The coming Messiah is seen as an ideal, blessed ruler who will restore the kingdom of Israel and gather the scattered people together. During the Roman occupation, from 63 BCE onwards, it was hoped that a Messiah would come to free them from political oppression. Hopes about the land are closely bound up with belief in the Messiah: he will restore the fortunes of Israel and bless the land.

Jesus of Nazareth claimed to be the Messiah, as many have throughout history. Many Jews rejected his claims as he was crucified and did not defeat Rome and bring in the kingdom of God. (Christians claim that he won a spiritual kingdom by dying on the cross and rising again.) Jesus is honoured as a holy rabbi by many contemporary Jews, though a minority accept him as Messiah, forming Messianic Jewish communities.

A pretender in more recent times was Shabbetai Zevi (1626–76), a Turkish Jew from Smyrna. He was a young rabbi who was born on the traditional birth date of the Messiah. He went to the Holy land and was hailed as Messiah by Nathan of Gaza, who styled himself as his prophet.

He returned to Turkey and gathered many followers. He spoke of organizing an army of Jews to reconquer the Holy Land, but when threatened with execution if he did not become a Muslim, he converted and most of his followers deserted him.

THE WORLD TO COME

Many Jews believe in a life after death as well as following the Ten Commandments here on earth. This belief developed gradually and is not clearly in the *Torah*. Gradually, the hope of not being left in the shadowy Underworld took hold, for God would not abandon his people in death. The God who made a covenant with them would see this through on the other side. There were hopes of being taken into glory, of seeing God, and these settled down into a belief in the resurrection of the body. Some passages of the Hebrew Bible might suggest that this hope is for a renewed, blessed earth. Other ideas are that this is a spiritual existence, a raising up into glory.

Judaism was the first religion to fully proclaim that people could enter the presence of God after death; in many pagan faiths, souls were kept in the Underworld, and only a few specially chosen ones made it into heaven. Judaism thus refers to *Olam Ha'Ba*, the 'World to Come'.

Paths to Peace

'The Lord blesses his people with peace.'

Psalm 29:11

DAILY PRAYER

Daily prayers involve reciting traditional Hebrew prayers such as the *Shema* as well as saying personal, spontaneous prayers. Some Orthodox Jewish men wear the *tefillin*, or phylacteries, leather boxes containing the *Shema* and Deuteronomy 6 that are strapped around the forehead and the arm. The Hebrew letter *shin* is on the boxes, and the straps on the head and arm form the shape of the letters *daled* and *yud* respectively, making the Hebrew word *Shaddai* for 'Almighty'. They are to remember the Law and to practise it – in the head and in the hand.

Judaism developed three daily times of prayer in the hands of the rabbis. Set prayer times were probably not known until the time of Ezra in the fifth century BCE. Before this, Jews would probably have prayed once a day, using their own words, but including the elements of praise, supplication and thanks.

The rabbis stressed that set prayers, the *siddur*, must be said with good intention and feeling. Rushing them by rote does not count. One needs to practise 'intention' or 'direction', *kavanah*. A first-century rabbi, Eliezer, said, 'When you pray, know before Whom you stand!'

A Jewish cemetery on the Mount of Olives.

TALLIT AND TZITZIT

Jews wear a prayer shawl called a *tallit*, covering the head when they pray. These have fringes, *tzitzit*, tied on them. The fringes were commanded in the *Torah* in Numbers 15:38:

> 'Throughout the generations to come you are to make tassels on the corners of your garments with a blue cord on each tassel. You will have these tassels to look at and so you will remember all the commands of the Lord...'

Orthodox Jewish men and boys will wear a *tallit katan,* an undershirt with tassels on, from dressing in the morning until they undress at night. A prayer will be recited: 'Blessed are you, Lord our God, Ruler of the Universe, who sanctified us with His commandments, and commanded us to wrap ourselves in *tzitzit.*'

A sacred place for the Jews is the Western Wall in Jerusalem. This is the only remaining wall of Herod's Temple, which was destroyed by the Romans in 70 CE. Jews will travel there on pilgrimage and pray in front of it. It is a visual and touchable reminder of their heritage, a piece of holy ground. Some write their prayers on scrolls and push them into the cracks in the wall.

ETHICS

'And God spoke all these words:

"I am the Lord your God, who brought you out of Egypt, out of the land of slavery.
"You shall have no other gods before me.
"You shall not make for yourself an idol in the form of anything in heaven above or on the earth beneath or in the waters below.
You shall not bow down to them or worship them; for I, the Lord your God, am a jealous God, punishing the children for the sin of the fathers to the third and fourth generation of those who hate me, but showing love to a thousand generations of those who love me and keep my commandments.
"You shall not misuse the name of the Lord your God, for the Lord will not hold anyone guiltless who misuses his name.
"Remember the Sabbath day by keeping it holy. Six days you shall labour and do all your work, but the seventh day is a Sabbath to the Lord your God. On it you shall not do any work, neither you, nor your son or daughter, nor your manservant or maidservant, nor your animals, nor the alien within your gates. For in six days the Lord made the heavens and the earth, the sea, and all that is in them, but he rested on the seventh day. Therefore the Lord blessed the Sabbath day and made it holy.
"Honour your father and your mother, so that you may live long in the land the Lord your God is giving you.
"You shall not murder.

Blessings

Jews recite a blessing, *b'rakhah*, on many different occasions, such as getting up and going to sleep, or before eating and drinking, or when hearing good news, or when seeing something wonderful in nature. Thus the blessing for bread is:

'Blessed are you, Lord our God, Ruler of the Universe, who brings forth bread from the earth.'

Or when seeing the ocean:

'Blessed are you, Lord our God, Ruler of the Universe, who made the great sea.'

The *Amidah* prayer is recited standing, morning and evening, and contains eighteen blessings. The book of Deuteronomy promises blessings upon Israel if they are obedient:

'All these blessings will come upon you and accompany you if you obey the Lord your God.'

Deuteronomy 28:2

The word for 'blessing', *b'rakhah*, comes from the same root as 'spring'. It is about life and well-being, refreshment and happiness.

"You shall not commit adultery.
"You shall not steal.
"You shall not give false testimony against your neighbour.
"You shall not covet your neighbour's house. You shall not covet your neighbour's wife, or his manservant or maidservant, his ox or donkey, or anything that belongs to your neighbour."

Exodus 20:1–17

A Jewish boy wearing the tefillin at daily prayers.

The Decalogue, the Ten Commandments, sums up the code of life for a Jew. These cover social and religious commandments. There are many other ethical guidelines in the Hebrew Scriptures, such as the holiness code in Leviticus 19, which includes the commandment:

> *'Do not curse the deaf or put a stumbling-block in front of the blind, but fear your God. I am the Lord.'*
>
> Leviticus 19:14

There are also summary passages, such as Micah 6:8.

> *'He has showed you, O man,*
>   *what is good.*
> *And what does the Lord require*
>   *of you?*
> *To act justly and to love mercy*
>   *and to walk humbly with your God.'*

The Hebrew prophets were not only concerned with foretelling events, but they spoke the word of God for their contemporaries, urging people to follow God's ethical commandments. Amos, for example, castigated the people for holding religious festivals when there was no justice in the land and a great divide between rich and poor. After 70 CE and the fall of the Temple, the rabbis said that righteous works replaced the sacrifices of old: God required mercy and a contrite heart more than sacrificial blood from animal offerings.

Awe and Wonder

> *'Shout for joy to the Lord, all the earth. Worship the Lord with gladness; come before him with joyful songs.'*
>
> Psalm 100:1

KIDDUSH AND THE HOME

The heart of Jewish worship is in the home. Whether daily, family prayers, or the weekly *Shabbat* meal, or annual festivals, the synagogue takes second place. *Kiddush* is a thanksgiving that is said over bread and wine to sanctify them, to set them apart for sacred use:

> *'Blessed are You, Lord our God, Ruler of the Universe, who brings forth bread from the earth... who creates the fruit of the vine.'*

The *Shabbat* gathers the family together for a shared meal. The Sabbath lights are lit before this by the mother, welcoming and honouring God's presence:

> *'Blessed are You, Lord our God, Ruler of the Universe, who sanctified us with your commandments and commanded us to kindle the lights of Shabbat.'*

The father then says the *Kiddush* over the bread and wine. The family greet each other with the words, *Shabbat shalom!* ('Peace on the Sabbath!')

The *Torah* commands Jews not to work on *Shabbat*. The word *Shabbat* means 'rest' and lasts from Friday evening until Saturday evening. Rabbis have debated what actually constitutes 'work' over the centuries, and the *Talmud* lists 39 forbidden categories from ploughing fields to carrying loads.

Orthodox Jews interpret this to the letter, having time switches for lights and preparing food the day before.

There is a balance in *Shabbat*; the rabbis have developed a poetic understanding of this, with *Shabbat* as a bride and as a queen. According to their parable, when the first week of creation was over, each day was named after its number (the days of the week are still so named in Hebrew today). Only *Shabbat* stood alone with a name or title. God gave *Shabbat* to Israel as a bride, to be loved and cherished. *Shabbat* is to be a delight as families gather together to celebrate. As queen, *Shabbat* rules and reminds Israel of the commandments, urging them to remember their Creator. The rabbis of the sixth to twelfth centuries CE developed a life-saving code, *pikuakh nefesh* ('saving a life'). A doctor must treat a patient, so a person must go to another's aid, breaking all the commandments of *Shabbat* for a greater, humanitarian good.

THE TEMPLE

The Hebrew Bible mentions the Temple as the focus of worship; Jews no longer have a Temple. The 'temple' began as a tent with a courtyard in the days of Moses. This was a series of poles and canvases that could be carried around by the tribes. When they had settled in the land, King Solomon built a permanent Temple in Jerusalem on Mount Zion. This was destroyed by the Babylonians in the sixth century BCE, which was seen as a great disaster. The Temple was rebuilt in the next century and modified and extended by Herod the Great in the first century CE. The Romans destroyed this in 70 CE. It has never been rebuilt.

The Synagogue

'Synagogue' is Greek for 'assembly'. The term is a sign that this was developed by Jews who lived away from Judea, scattered in communities all over the Mediterranean. They could not easily travel to the Temple in Jerusalem, and weekly assemblies gathered to study the *Torah* and to praise God. The layout of the synagogue is simple. There is a cupboard, the ark, at the front, with a seven-branched candlestick to one side. This is the *menorah*. A reader's desk stands in the middle, with seating arranged around this. The ark contains scrolls of the *Torah*; the *menorah* represents the seven days of creation, and the candlelight suggests the presence of the living God. The desk is the *bimah*, from where the service is led and where the scrolls are laid out and read from. The basic structure will intersperse prayers with Psalms, the *Torah* reading and final prayers for the government of the land and the state of Israel. The *Torah* will then be replaced in the ark.

In Orthodox synagogues, men and women sit separately. The procession of the *Torah* scrolls around the synagogue to the *bimah* is a joyful time, and people reach out to kiss the scrolls or to touch them with their prayer books which they then kiss.

Orthodox services are all in Hebrew; Reform ones have a mixture, often about 75 per cent Hebrew and 25 per cent English. Some prayers and chants, such as the *Shema*, are always in Hebrew.

Following spread: Members of a Hasidic Jewish family.

The Temple had elaborate symbolism with golden fittings and artwork, many lights and clouds of sweet-smelling incense. An altar stood in front of the Holy Place, the innermost chamber. There, offerings of grain or animals were brought. This might be in thanksgiving or for atonement, dealing with sin. The *Torah* instructed that blood had to be shed and sprinkled on the altar to cover sin, a life for a life as it were. In the Holy Place was a table with bread laid before God, and the ark of the covenant. This contained the tablets of the Law. It was lost at some point, possibly when the first Temple was destroyed. The Holy Place was empty by Roman times.

Temple worship taught much about the holiness and majesty of God and gave ritual ways to approach him and to be purified. There was an array of musicians and chanting. It was visual, dramatic and energetic. This tradition was lost, but the reverence for the *Torah* and the reciting of Psalms of praise continue in the synagogues and at major festivals.

The rabbis taught that prayer and almsgiving, doing works of mercy, had replaced the Temple offerings.

Journey into Mystery

'Teach them to your children, talking about them when you sit at home and when you walk along the road, when you lie down and when you get up.'

THE *MEZUZAH*

The *mezuzah* contains a small scroll of part of Deuteronomy 6 and 11, being the *Shema* and the command to wear the laws on the head and the hand. The *mezuzah* is always fixed on the outer door of a house, and often on every door within except for the toilet, the bathroom and the garage. *Mezuzahs* are attached to

Inside the synagogue, showing the opened scroll of the Torah.

rooms of residence. They are fixed diagonally and Jews touch these with reverence as they enter.

Judaism tends to be very much a religion of the book, of the word, but it uses symbols and rituals to reinforce the message. Bread and wine, candles, seven-branched candlesticks and decorated scrolls can all be pressed into service for spiritual illumination.

CIRCUMCISION

Jewish males have a rite of passage to induct them into the covenant community: circumcision became the sign of the covenant very early in the development of the Jewish faith. Abraham instituted this by divine

command, according to the *Torah*. Many Near Eastern tribes practised circumcision, but as a coming-of-age ceremony during puberty. Jews did – and still do – this much earlier, usually eight days after a child's birth.

The child is brought in to joyful acclaims from the family as they shout 'Blessed is he!' A rabbi places the child on a cushion known as 'the throne', and either he or a specially trained person (a *mohel*) performs the circumcision. The child's father takes him in his arms and says, 'Blessed are You, Lord our God, Ruler of the Universe, who has sanctified us with his commandments and commanded us to enter my son into the covenant of Abraham.'

BAR MITZVAH AND BAT MITZVAH

Jews have a coming-of-age ceremony: *Bar Mitzvah* means 'Son of the commandment' and *Bat Mitzvah* means 'Daughter of the commandment'. Orthodox Jews allow only boys to undergo this at the age of 13; Reform Jews allow girls to have a Bat Mitzvah at age 12. The young people have to learn Hebrew and recite a passage from the *Torah*. In Orthodox Judaism, a boy is then treated as a man in religious matters, and he can form part of the *minyan*, the minimum number of ten men needed to start a synagogue.

MIRACLES

Jews believe that miracles can happen and that holy men and women can perform them by God's blessing. They are rare and exceptional, but possible. Miracles are special signs of God's reality. They might not always be supernatural,

'One cannot look directly at God just as one cannot look at a solar eclipse without a filter; the *Sefirot* are filters to help us look at God, the majestic, mysterious One.'
A Kabbalist from New York

'I was very nervous at my *Bat Mitzvah*. I had practised my Hebrew reading for days and I was afraid of stumbling over the words. There was a great sense of elation and calm afterwards. Then I really knew that I belonged.'
Esther, a Jewish girl from Haifa

'Anyone who believes all the stories of miracles performed by the masters is a fool; anyone who says that they cannot have happened is an unbeliever.'
Hasidic Jewish saying

✳

using natural forces that were once not understood by ancient minds, but they have the hand of God within them. In the first century CE, for example, there were some holy men said to heal the sick and bring answers to prayer, such as rain in a drought. Jesus is sometimes seen by modern Jews against this background.

Making Merry

'Celebrate the Feast of Unleavened Bread, because it was on this very day that I brought your divisions out of Egypt. Celebrate this day as a lasting ordinance for the generations to come.'

Exodus 12:17

A Jewish boy reads the Scriptures in Hebrew for his Bar Mitzvah.

PESACH

Pesach (Passover) is a spring festival that follows the lunar calendar, so its date varies each year in the solar calendar. It often coincides with the date of the Christian Easter celebrations. *Pesach* begins on the Jewish date of 15 *Nisan* and lasts for seven days, or eight for Jews outside Israel. The name *Pesach* recalls both the paschal lamb that was offered in the old Jerusalem Temple on the eve of the festival, and the idea of God passing over (*pasach* in Hebrew) the Israelites' homes and smiting the Egyptians before Moses led the Hebrews out of slavery.

The biblical name is *Chag Ha-Matzot*, 'the Festival of Unleavened Bread'. This is because the Hebrews were commanded to eat unleavened bread for the seven days of the festival.

After the destruction of the Temple in 70 CE, the paschal lamb could not be offered any more, and so the celebration focused entirely on the meal in the home. The meal follows an order, the *Seder*, and there are various symbolic foods assembled on the table as well as ordinary food. The biblical *Pesach* had unleavened bread and roasted lamb with bitter herbs. This has been extended to include a roasted egg, salt water, *charoseth* – a mixture of apple, nuts, wine and cinnamon – and parsley. These all have symbolic meanings and can be referred to or eaten during the *Seder*:

* roasted egg – new life coming from destruction
* salt water – the tears of the slaves
* *charoseth* – the joy and sweetness of freedom
* parsley – new life and provision for the Hebrews on their journey

Mysticism

Symbols and words can convey a sense of transcendence and mystery: Jews worship a God who is beyond, wholly other than the world, yet the Hebrew prophets often had an overpowering sense of his presence. After the end of prophecy in Judaism, many rabbis sought a direct encounter with the divine, or hidden mysteries in the *Torah*. There are many types of mysticism in world faiths. Judaism tends to downplay the idea that the soul can feel absorbed by God and at one with the divine, but there are many movements that seek to enter further into divine mystery.

The *Kabbalah* is a school of Jewish mysticism that has been popularized by media stars in recent years, but it contains rituals and wisdom teaching as well as the mystical. It is only one Jewish school of mysticism: there were others before it and after it. *Kabbalah* means 'tradition' and claims to be the secret teaching of the *Torah*, going back to Moses and even as far as Adam. It is also called 'secret wisdom', *hokhma nistarah*. There are two Kabbalistic schools, the Zohar of the twelfth century CE and the Lurianic of the sixteenth century. The latter was an elaboration of the former. The Zohar began with Isaac the Blind in Provence and then spread to Spain where it was refined and became popular.

The *Kabbalah* mixes pagan Greek ideas with esoteric Judaism. Basically, God has two aspects – God in himself and God in his revelation. The former is En Sof, the Infinite. En Sof is unknowable, but he/it is made manifest through a series of ten emanations called *Sefirot,* which descend into the world and reach their pinnacle with human beings. Our behaviour affects the *Sefirot* and sinful behaviour interrupts the flow of divine blessing. To a Kabbalist, humans literally are holding up the heavens; we have the power to bring blessing or destruction. Orthodox and Reform Jews are divided on what to make of the *Kabbalah*; some accept it with reservations and some completely reject it.

'Strangers are invited to the *Pesach*; anyone is welcome as a guest. We especially want to allow all Jews to celebrate the festival, people who might be alone without their family.'

Miriam, a Jewish mother

The eldest son will ask his father 'Why is this night not like other nights?' and the father will begin to tell the story of Moses, the Hebrew slaves and the exodus. This story forms the *Haggadah* ('the Telling').

A glass of wine will be left for the prophet Elijah, in the hope that he might return before the end of the meal, and a final toast prays, 'Next year in Jerusalem! Next year may all be free!'

Jews believe that they are in the presence of the living God when they celebrate *Pesach*, the same God who set the slaves free centuries earlier. Thus the hope of deliverance from present misfortune is expressed at the end.

SHAVUOT

Shavuot is a summer festival. This remembers the giving of the *Torah* on Mount Sinai. Synagogues are decorated with many flowers. *Shavuot* means 'Feast of Weeks'. It occurs seven weeks after the *Pesach* and was originally a spring harvest festival. As this time was coincidental with the Hebrews arriving at Mount Sinai, the rabbis developed the festival more in this way. Dairy products are eaten at *Shavuot*, possibly symbolizing the milk of the *Torah* that nourishes. Another name for the festival is Pentecost.

SUKKOT

Sukkot means 'huts', and it is an autumn festival that recalls the time spent by the Hebrews living in tents in the desert before they entered Canaan. Jews build shelters in their gardens and decorate these. In hotter climates such as Israel's, families might sleep in them; otherwise just meals will be eaten in them. This is to be done for seven days.

Simchat Torah

Simchat Torah means 'rejoicing in the *Torah*'. People gather at the synagogue and the scrolls of the *Torah* are carried around the synagogue seven times. People sing and dance for joy. Jewish worship can be exuberant and energetic, rather than solemn and word based all the time. Circle dancing is often used as people link arms and dance in circles to hymns and folk songs. This follows feelings in the Psalms about rejoicing and delighting in God's Law:

'Oh, how I love your law! I meditate on it all day long.'

Psalm 119:97

These three festivals are mentioned in the Hebrew Bible as pilgrimage festivals, when people were expected to come to Jerusalem.

HANNUKAH

Hannukah remembers the time when the Jewish faith was nearly destroyed by the Syrians in the second century BCE, when Greek culture was imposed upon Judea by the conquering king, Antiochus. A group of freedom fighters was led by Judas Maccabeus. They defeated the invaders and drove them out. The Temple had been desecrated with a statue of Zeus erected inside. The temple was cleansed and dedicated once more to the worship of God. *Hannukah* means 'dedication'. The seven-branched candlestick, the *menorah*, was brought back into the Temple, but there was only enough oil to burn it for one night. It would take eight days to get more. Somehow, the candle burned for eight days, and so *Hannukah* lasts for eight days. It uses a *Hannukah menorah* which has eight candles, one being lit each day. Presents are given as part of the celebrations.

There are many more Jewish festivals, including *Rosh Hashannah*, the New Year celebration, *Yom Kippur*, the Day of Atonement when people ask for forgiveness, and *Purim*, which celebrates deliverance from persecution in the time of Queen Esther.

Today

> *'See, I am doing a new thing! Now it springs up, do you perceive it?'*
>
> Isaiah 43:19

REFORM AND TRADITION

Judaism has had various schools of thought from the beginning with different emphases and practices. After 70 CE, the Pharisee party was dominant, with its trained rabbis and codification of traditions in the *Talmud*. This emerged as Orthodox Judaism. Some have sought to accommodate Jewish practice in the societies in which they lived. The nineteenth century saw the rise of Reform Judaism, which went a stage further and adapted the synagogue services, using the vernacular to a degree and simplifying religious dress. Men and women sat together and came to be regarded as equals. Some women rabbis now practise in Reform congregations.

The basic issue is whether Judaism is a given, with the *Torah's* commandments being complete and unchangeable for all time, or whether it has developed over the centuries with different insights that are more appropriate to different times. Reform Jews accept that a core of the *Torah* came from Moses himself; Orthodox Jews believe all 613 commandments were given to Moses on Mount Sinai.

The eight branches Hannukah candlestick.

The land

Hopes for the land were in the faith from the days of Abraham and the Patriarchs. The story unfolds in the Hebrew Bible where the people lose their land and go into exile, only to be returned years later by the Persians. The northern tribes of Israel were lost entirely, though, when they went into exile at the hand of Assyria. The Romans conquered Jerusalem and put down rebellions in the first and second centuries CE. Few Jews lived in the region after this and it became known as 'Palestine'. Jews lived in scattered communities throughout the world. There were longings for a return as expressed in the medieval songs of Judah Halevi, but the idea of using political means emerged in the nineteenth century. Zionism was the movement to win back the Jewish homeland, led by Theodore Herzl. Some Reform Jews were suspicious of the new movement, as it denied universalism, the idea that all people were equal before God. The Orthodox rejected it because it denied the Messiah; in traditional belief the Messiah would lead the Jews back to their homeland. It was the experience of the Holocaust and the formation of the State of Israel in 1948 that turned the tide and threw many different Jewish groups behind the nation.

Hopes for peace are still dim with conflicts between Palestinian Arabs and Jews continuing. Some Palestinians had been settled in the land for generations and some were recent arrivals when the new nation of Israel was formed. Tensions about where borders should lie and new settlements still create security problems. Israel did not have control of Jerusalem until June 1967 when it was taken in the Six Day War. There are Christian and Muslim sections to this day, but Israel has overall control again.

Further subdivisions occurred such as Liberal Progressive Judaism. Conservative Jews are closer to Orthodoxy, but wish to make some concessions to reform.

Hasidic Judaism is a more mystical branch of the religion, founded by Rabbi Baal Shem Tov (1700–60). Their leaders are thought to have greater spiritual gifts and insights than formally trained rabbis.

MESSIAH

Many have been the hopes, beliefs and legends around this figure throughout the history of Judaism. Some have emphasized the Messianic Age more than the man, an age of blessing and peace that is to come. The Orthodox hold to a personal Messiah, and the Reform have more fluid views. Many see the Messiah as a symbol of the possibility of a better future and widespread aid and education. Some Reform Jews call their synagogues 'temples', as they have replaced the Temple.

JEWS AROUND THE WORLD

The largest community of Jews is not in Israel (about 4,700,000) but in the USA (about 5,900,000). Smaller communities exist around the world such as 600,000 in France, 550,000 in Russia, 260,000 in the UK and 250,000 in Argentina. The problem faced by Jews in various countries is assimilation, losing their distinctiveness and blending with the community. In the USA, for example, fewer than 50 per cent of Jews go to a synagogue and more than 40 per cent marry outside the faith.

PERSECUTION

The figure of the 'wandering Jew' is present in medieval literature, cursed to wander the earth and never settle in their homeland because of their rejection of Christ. Sadly, the medieval church taught that the Jews were 'Christ-killers' guilty of deicide, even though Jesus was a Jew, Paul was a Jew, and so were the twelve Apostles. This was contrary to the New Testament, where Jews are honoured as the root of the tree of faith that the gentile Christians had been grafted onto. There were periodic outbursts of persecution and pogroms as far apart as York in England and Tsarist Russia. Medieval Jews had to wear distinctive clothing and a yellow star. Hitler revived the yellow star and embarked upon a vicious campaign of genocide, as new technology and ruthless planning were used to exterminate the Jews from Europe. The Holocaust, or the *Shoah*, destroyed about 6 million Jews. This experience drove people to try to return to Israel to seek a safe and permanent homeland.

A memorial stands at Yad Vashem in Israel to all who were killed in the *Shoah*, and an eternal flame burns in their memory. Anti-Semitism is not as widespread as it was, but it still rears its head as one form of racism today.

JUDAISM — at a glance...

- When did it begin?– Orthodox Jews would trace their faith to the dawn of time with the first man, Adam. The prophet Abraham lived c. 1700 BCE, and Moses c. 1400–1200 BCE.
- The founder – There is no single founder, though Moses takes on a role closest to that as he receives the *Torah* on Mount Sinai.
- God – God is known as El or Yahweh and is eternal and transcendent.
- Redeemer figure – The prophets, such as Moses, are just teachers. There is the hope of the Messiah, though. Some passages suggest that he will suffer for the people or will bring in the kingdom of God.
- Scriptures – The *Tenakh*, the Hebrew Bible, is a collection of 39 books, split up into the three sections of the *Torah*, the Prophets and the Writings.
- Beliefs – Jews believe that God has called them to follow his commandments in the *Torah* and has bound them to him in a covenant. They are to be a light to the nations. The blessings of the covenant are not for this life only, but also for the world to come.
- Place of worship – Originally the home and the Temple in Jerusalem, where many offerings and sacrifices were made. This was destroyed in 70 CE, and by then local meeting places, synagogues, had been established.
- Sacred food – The *Torah* prohibits various foods such as pork and shellfish. Jewish tradition will not allow meat and milk to be eaten together. Bread and wine are often used at prayer times and festivals.
- Main festivals – *Pesach* includes a family meal with symbolic foods that recall the exodus from Egypt. *Sukkot* has people erecting shelters to remember the days in the wilderness. *Simchat Torah* rejoices in the giving of the *Torah*. *Hannukah* is a festival of light.
- Key Symbols – The Star of David; the seven-branched *menorah* remembers creation.

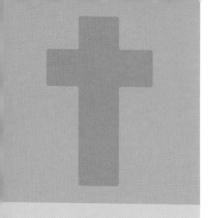

Christianity

'For God so loved the world that he gave his one and only Son, that whoever believes in him shall not perish but have eternal life.'

John 3:16

GOD AND MAN

Christianity is a faith based upon 'the Christ', believed to be Jesus of Nazareth. Jesus was a Jew who lived in the first century CE. Christians believe that he was God and man at the same time, a sublime unity of heaven and earth.

YESHUA

Jesus, Yeshua in Aramaic, would have been known as Yeshua Bar Yosif, Jesus son of Joseph. 'Christ' was a special title, a Greek term, the same as 'Messiah' in Hebrew. This means 'anointed king'. Joseph soon drops out of the story in the Gospels, creating the assumption that he died early. Later traditions state that he was much older than Mary, who would have been a teenager when they were married. The same traditions disclose that the brothers and sisters of Jesus mentioned in the Bible were in fact step-siblings from Joseph's former marriage and that he was a widower. However, we are told none of this in the Gospels.

Joseph is said to have been a *tekton* in the Greek language. This could mean carpenter, joiner or even builder. We presume that Jesus carried on in the family business until he became a wandering teacher. This must have caused his family some consternation, as hinted at in Mark 3:21:

> 'When his family heard about this, they went to take charge of him, for they said, "He is out of his mind."'

THE HOLY LAND IN THE FIRST CENTURY

The Jews settled in two areas, Galilee in the north and Judea in the south. These were separated by Samaria, the land of an immigrant race who were settled there centuries earlier by the Assyrians. Judea held the capital city, Jerusalem, and was the more prosperous area. Galilee was a cluster of small towns and villages, which bordered onto gentile zones where large, affluent Roman cities could be found. The Galileans would have found work in the pagan cities as artisans. Jesus' Galilean homeland was poor, largely built on farming and craft for hire.

In a nutshell

Christianity began as a Jewish movement in the Middle East. Jesus was a Galilean Jew who lived in a backwater of the Roman empire, between around 4 BCE and 33 CE. The faith he inspired spread throughout the empire, eventually winning out as its official faith in the fourth century CE. Centuries of emperor worship and pagan pantheons were discarded in favour of the prophet and carpenter from the East. The faith also reached ancient Persia, China and India, but its main roots were in North Africa, the Greek world and what would become known as Europe.

Christianity is a faith built upon paradox. It claims not only that God could become man but also that a crucified man would be hailed as Saviour and Lord. Crucifixion was a barbaric punishment for common criminals and rebels in the Roman empire and to die such a death was a scandal. But Christians believe that one who appeared to fail so ignobly later became highly exalted. Christianity revolves around the concept of humility, forgiveness and divine grace – unmerited favour.

'The Word became flesh and made his dwelling among us.'
John 1:14

✳

The ascended Jesus.

The genius

Christians would sum up the genius of their faith thus: God stepped into his creation like an author writing himself into his novel. He stepped in not just to teach the right path or to illumine minds with heavenly wisdom, but to save or redeem the world. God came to earth to die upon a cross for the sins of the world, and to rise again to victory. The genius of Christianity is that the world has a Redeemer: God himself, in the flesh.

The symbol

The chief Christian symbol is a cross, in memory of the crucifixion of Christ. For many Christians an empty cross is a reminder that the story of Jesus did not end with his death, but with his resurrection to new life.

Christ healing the sick.

First Steps

'In the sixth month, God sent the angel Gabriel to Nazareth, a town in Galilee, to a virgin pledged to be married to a man named Joseph, a descendant of David. The virgin's name was Mary.'

Luke 1:26-27

WHERE DID IT BEGIN?

Nazareth, the village where Jesus was brought up, must have been particularly small as archeologists have found few graves there. The Gospels reveal that Nazareth was held with a certain degree of scorn as a small-minded, one-horse sort of place. When the disciple Nathaniel was told that Jesus wanted to speak to him, he muttered, 'Nazareth! Can anything good come from there?' (John 1:46).

JESUS

Joseph is said not to have been the actual father of Jesus, but an adoptive one. Mary was pregnant before they were married, and not by him. The custom then, as it can be today in some Middle Eastern cultures, was to have the girl put to death as she would have been a disgrace to the family. He resolved to have her betrothal agreement rescinded quietly, in order to spare her life. Something made him relent, and he married her and raised the child as his own. The Gospel of Matthew describes a dream in which an angel spoke to him.

Both Matthew's Gospel and Luke's Gospel claim that Jesus was born of a virgin, though the rest of the New Testament is silent about this. However, there is a hint that Jesus was held to be illegitimate by his opponents: 'Then they asked him, "Where is your father?"' (John 8:19). (Later pagan writers scoffed that Jesus must have been sired by a Roman soldier, something for which there is no evidence at all.) The virgin birth is seen as a miracle, showing the power of God to create life directly in the womb, bypassing the normal laws of biology. Most Christians down the ages have believed this wholeheartedly, and it is enshrined in the Christian Creeds. Some people today, however, wonder whether the virgin birth could be metaphorical, symbolic of the spiritual power and presence of God at work in Jesus.

 Jesus' ministry

The Gospels give us a loose framework of Jesus' ministry; this is summed up in the preaching of the apostles in the Acts of the Apostles, such as Peter's speech to Cornelius:

We are witnesses of everything he did in the country of the Jews and in Jerusalem. They killed him by hanging him on a tree, but God raised him from the dead on the third day and caused him to be seen. He was not seen by all the people, but by witnesses whom God had already chosen – by us who ate and drank with him after he rose from the dead. He commanded us to preach to the people and to testify that he is the one whom God appointed as judge of the living and the dead. All the prophets testify about him that everyone who believes in him receives forgiveness of sins through his name.'
Acts 10:34–36

After Jesus was baptized by John the Baptist, he ministered in Galilee, and then went back to Judea where he ended his days in Jerusalem.

The fourth Gospel, John, presents a different chronology which is intriguing. Jesus visits Jerusalem and ministers there three times, between work in Galilee.

The Gospels string together collections of sayings, parables and healing stories around this simple framework. We are told few exact dates, but Jesus is anchored firmly in history in the reign of Tiberius Caesar, when Pontius Pilate was procurator of Judea. This places his life in the first part of the first century CE, and his death in around 33 CE.

However long Jesus lived, whatever the exact dates, the story did not end there. The early Christians related his resurrection, a bursting forth into new life, after the cross. Most Jews hoped for a resurrection of the dead at the end of time, but this man had stepped into it before anyone else. This, they thought, proclaimed him as Lord and Saviour.

SON OF DAVID

There are certain themes interwoven throughout the birth stories about Davidic ancestry. The Jews hoped for a new king, a descendant of David, a chosen leader anointed as king, or 'Messiah' in Hebrew. This Davidic hope plays through the Old Testament prophets and is picked up in the Gospels and the rest of the New Testament. Jesus was hailed as a 'Son of David'. This Old Testament hope can be traced to many of the psalms, such as Psalm 89:3–4:

> 'I have made a covenant with my chosen one, I have sworn to David my servant, I will establish your line forever and make your throne firm through all generations.'

The early preaching of Jesus' first followers, the apostles, echoes these ideas. The Davidic hope is referred to several times in the New Testament and Jesus is seen as the fulfilment of this.

'SON'?

Jesus carries three 'Son' titles in the Gospels – Son of David, Son of Man and Son of God. The 'Son of Man' (meaning 'human being') was a Messianic title based upon a vision of a coming Saviour in the book of Daniel. 'Son of God' could carry many levels of meaning. It could denote the Jewish king, as in the psalms (for example, Psalm 2:7: 'He said to me, "You are my Son; today I have become your Father." '). It could mean a holy man, and Israel as a whole was called 'son' in Hosea 11:1: 'out of Egypt I called my son'. For the early church, it also meant that Jesus was uniquely close to God. Later, the title came to mean the part of God who took flesh, 'the Son'.

The Goal

> 'Whoever does not love does not know God, because God is love.'
>
> 1 John 4:8

THE TRINITY

Christians are believers in one God, or monotheists, but they talk about there being three parts to God: the Father, the Son and the Holy Spirit. This is the doctrine of the Trinity. Perhaps it is bit like the way H_2O exists in three forms: water, steam and ice. One object *can* exist in three ways. But Christians believe that God is personal and not a force or an inanimate thing. So just as we humans are not fully alive as isolated individuals, but only in relation to one another, so Christians believe there is a dynamic movement within God's being: God is interrelational.

GOD AS FATHER

The 'Father' aspect of God suggests a Creator. Philosophers speak of the First Cause of the cosmos or the Unmoved Mover. The picture that might come to mind is of vast galaxies of tiny stars and interstellar space. God is transcendent and beyond.

Yet the title 'Father' speaks to Christians of love, personality, and overarching care and protection. Jesus sometimes used an intimate term for 'Father', *Abba* in his native Aramaic, when praying to God. This was a term of affection that a child would use to address its father.

There is a deep irony and paradox in calling God 'Father'; it combines vastness and mystery with intimate love. Some tend to think of God as an old man in

The developing message

The doctrine of the Trinity was fully worked out by the Church Fathers, being affirmed strongly in the Nicene Creed (325 CE). Yet the basic concept was there early on in the New Testament. The threefold nature of God is seen in the early Christian prayer, 'The Grace':

'May the grace of our Lord Jesus Christ, and the love of God and the fellowship of the Holy Spirit be with us all, evermore. Amen.'
2 Corinthians 13:13

The Christians experienced God in this way. It was not just an abstract idea. Traces of belief in the Trinity can be seen in passages of the Gospels, such as the baptism of Jesus. The Father speaks, Jesus is the Son, and the Spirit descends:

'As soon as Jesus was baptized, he went up out of the water. At that moment heaven was opened, and he saw the Spirit of God descending like a dove and lighting on him. And a voice from heaven said, "This is my Son, whom I love; with him I am well pleased"'
Matthew 3:16–17

This same, threefold dynamic can be seen at work in the story of the stoning of Stephen, the first martyr, in Acts 7:55: 'But Stephen, full of the Holy Spirit, looked up into heaven and saw the glory of God, and Jesus standing at the right hand of God...': God (that is, the Father), Jesus, Holy Spirit are all involved.

'For you did not receive a spirit that makes you a slave again to fear, but the Spirit of sonship. And by him we cry, "Abba, Father."'
Romans 8:15

'...God Himself is a society. It is indeed a fathomless mystery of theology... This triple enigma is as comforting as wine and as open as an English fireside; this thing that bewilders the intellect utterly quietens the heart.'
G. K. Chesterton, ***Orthodoxy***

❊

the sky with a white beard. For Christians, however, God is invisible Spirit and not a force that is 'out there'.

GOD AS SON

The 'Son' is the aspect of God that is also called the 'Word' or 'Wisdom' in the New Testament. These descriptions suggest that he is a God who is 'down here', actively involved in the world.

The New Testament hails Jesus as the 'Word' and the 'Wisdom' of God. Thus a huge leap is made between Old and New Testaments. The Word or the Wisdom became human and lived among his people.

Jesus was also called the 'Son' of God, and Christians believe that he is God incarnate. This is a title that is rich in meaning in the Bible, but after Jesus' resurrection Christians understood it as a confirmation of Jesus' divine nature and status. He was part of God, and he had now returned to God.

THE HOLY SPIRIT

The Holy Spirit is also seen as an expression of God. Christians believe that the Spirit makes people holy and gives life. In the New Testament, the Spirit is pictured as, among other things, wind, water and fire. The wind is invisible and unpredictable, but you can see its effects. Water gives life and refreshes. Fire gives light and purifies.

Theologians see the Spirit revealed in the human faces of ordinary believers who are touched by light and joy. They are the 'face' of the Spirit.

THE ROUND DANCE

Later Church Fathers taught that the three Persons of the Trinity were eternally joined in a round dance of love, the one living in the other. They were coequal. They were one God. Eastern Christians developed an icon tradition to depict the mysterious Trinity. They referred to the story of Abraham and Sarah being visited by three strangers (to be found in the Old Testament in Genesis 18:1–15). These were seen as angels, and later as types of the persons of the Trinity. They were shown seated around the table, sharing the meal Sarah offered them. They were equal in size and importance. The table was open, inviting each onlooker to join their circle of fellowship.

Teachers of the Way

'They devoted themselves to the apostles' teaching and to the fellowship, to the breaking of bread and to prayer.'

Acts 2:42

THE WAY

The early Christian movement was known as 'the Way' before the term 'Christian' was coined. The first leaders and pastors were the apostles. The term 'apostle' comes from a Greek word meaning to be sent out. In their Near Eastern culture, a teacher or an official would send out his representatives who carried his authority. The apostles had been authorized to build the church by the risen Lord Jesus:

An icon of the visit of three angels to Abraham. They are seen as symbols of the Trinity.

THE TWELVE

The apostles were known as disciples at first. This means 'students' or 'followers'. They were called together by Jesus in his earthly ministry. There were twelve main men, symbolizing the twelve tribes of Israel.

The Gospels reveal their failings and their disputes, and their inability to grasp what their Master was teaching at times.

THE TRADITION OF THE APOSTLES

The first Christians only had the Old Testament as Scripture. There were traditions about Jesus, and early collections of his sayings and miracles (probably orally transmitted at first). The four Gospels as we know them took shape gradually and were established by the end of the first century. Some even suggest that they were all written before 70 CE.

Besides the words of Jesus and the insights of the Old Testament, there was the teaching of the apostles. All of this was clustered together to form a tradition, a precious body of teaching and truth, which was to be guarded and handed down.

The apostle Paul.

THE BIBLE

Christian Bibles contain the 39 books of the Old Testament and the 27 books of the New. The meaning of the word 'Testament' is the same as 'covenant', God's special agreement and binding promises to his people. The New Testament is about God's commitment to humanity through Jesus.

Influential Christians

Paul

Paul the apostle had not been a follower of Jesus during his lifetime. In fact, as a zealous Pharisee he had persecuted the early church. While on his way to Damascus to seek to prosecute Christians there, he had a stunning vision of Jesus in a bright light that blinded him temporarily. He accepted Christianity, was baptized, and settled in Antioch in Syria for some time. There he helped to lead the church. Eventually, he taught the faith to non-Jews, Gentiles, across the Roman world. He went to the local Jewish communities first, often winning converts from Gentiles who attended synagogue worship and who were known as 'God-fearers'.

Francis of Assisi

Francis Bernardone (1181/2–1226) was the son of a wealthy cloth merchant in Assisi in Italy. Serving as a soldier, he was captured and held for some months, during which he went through a deep conversion. He left the business, famously stripping himself naked and handing his clothes back to his father, and embraced poverty. He wore a simple habit and gathered other brothers around him. These were to follow the monastic vows of poverty, chastity and obedience, but they were to travel freely, preaching and teaching. The Pope gave his blessing on the new order in 1209–10 and it grew much larger than Francis ever imagined. He embraced lepers in the street who were shunned by everyone else, tamed a wild wolf who sat meekly at his feet as he made the sign of the cross, and made a peaceful mission to the Saracen Muslims during the violence of the Crusades.

Martin Luther

Luther (1483–1546) was an Augustinian friar at the University of Wittenberg in Saxony. He became vicar of his order in 1515, having charge of eleven monasteries. He had an experience of mercy and forgiveness sometime between 1512 and 1515 which convinced him that humans cannot earn the love of God but that God came in Christ to shift the burden of guilt from humanity. He started to question some of the church teachings of his day, and posted his 95 Theses on the door of Wittenberg Cathedral, trying to start a local debate. His main attack on the leadership of the church was the sale of indulgences, pardons from sin that freed souls to enter heaven. Unwittingly, he sparked off a movement called the Reformation that divided the church in Europe. The Reformers wished to purify the church and take it back to the days of the apostles. After years of division, the Roman Catholic Church and the Lutherans entered into a fruitful dialogue at the end of the twentieth century, and Luther himself has been affirmed as an honest, searching teacher of the Gospel.

The New Testament contains:

† four Gospels about Jesus

† the Acts of the Apostles about the first Christians

† 21 letters (or 'epistles') written by the apostles Paul, Peter and John

† the Revelation (or Apocalypse), a prophetic book about the end times.

DEVOTIONAL READING

For Christians, the Scriptures are a living source of teaching. They do not just record ancient history. To them, the Bible is inspired, God-breathed. There are debates about the manner of inspiration, and how much is factual and how much is symbolic. Should the Adam and Eve story be taken as history or as a parable? Are there understandable errors of science and history in the book, whilst its spiritual teachings are free from error? Whatever views are held, believers use the Scriptures devotionally, following the advice given in 1 Peter 2:2: 'Like newborn babes, crave pure spiritual milk, so that by it you may grow up in your salvation…'.

Treasury of the Heart

'…no-one can say, "Jesus is Lord", except by the Holy Spirit.'

Paul, 1 Corinthians 12:3

THE FOUNT AND THE TREASURE

The Christian faith is based upon the tradition that was handed down from the apostles. This is understood to be something precious, like a great treasure that is honoured and prized. It is also believed to be more than just a static list of abstract ideas or moral codes; it gives life. The tradition is like a gushing spring of the Spirit, a fountain of life and blessing that people swim and move in. Jesus had said that he would give people 'living water' and that this gift would spring up from within them. The tradition nurtures, guides and forms the believer.

An Ethiopian deacon studies the Bible.

'Indeed, the water I give him will become in him a spring of water welling up to eternal life.'

Jesus, John 4:14

AFFIRMATIONS

The early church seems to have developed various statements of belief for its new members. These might be very short, such as 'Jesus is Lord.' This would be a counterblast to the cult of emperor worship, where a sacrifice was offered to Caesar with the confession 'Caesar is Lord!' The New Testament has traces of other confessions, such as in 1 Timothy 3:16:

Playing in the waters of a fountain – water is a potent symbol in the New Testament of cleansing and refreshing.

'Beyond all question, the mystery
    of godliness is great:
He appeared in a body,
    was vindicated by the Spirit, was
seen by angels,
    was preached among the nations,
was believed on in the world,
    was taken up in glory.'

There is what looks like a baptismal blessing in Ephesians 5:14:

'Wake up, O sleeper,
rise from the dead,
and Christ will shine on you.'

CREEDS

Gradually, longer lists were composed of key Christian beliefs which circulated around the churches and became widespread. The Apostles' Creed is one of the earliest, having originated to teach converts preparing for baptism. Later creeds were devised by Church Councils, a general assembly of bishops with the Emperor who met to debate some disputed areas of doctrine and practice. The most common of these later creeds, still recited in modern church worship is the Nicene Creed. This was composed at the Council of Nicaea in 325 CE. If the two are compared, it will be seen that the latter has far more to say about who Jesus was. Both creeds focus on the Trinity: God is Creator, Jesus is the Redeemer, and the Holy Spirit is active in the Church.

THE APOSTLES' CREED

'I believe in God, the Father almighty,
*   creator of heaven and earth.*
I believe in Jesus Christ, his only
*   Son, our Lord,*
who was conceived by the Holy Spirit,
*   born of the Virgin Mary,*
suffered under Pontius Pilate,
*   was crucified, died, and was buried;*
*   he descended to the dead.*
On the third day he rose again;
*   ascended into heaven,*
he is seated at the right hand
*   of the Father,*
and he will come to judge the living
and the dead.

I believe in the Holy Spirit,
the holy catholic Church,
the communion of saints,

the forgiveness of sins,
the resurrection of the body,
and the life everlasting.
Amen.'

THE NICENE CREED

'We believe in one God,
The Father, the Almighty,
maker of heaven and earth,
of all that is, seen and unseen.

We believe in one Lord, Jesus Christ,
the only Son of God,
eternally begotten of the Father,
God from God, Light from Light,
true God from true God,
begotten, not made,
of one Being with the Father;
through him all things were made.
For us and for our salvation he came
*   down from heaven,*
was incarnate of the Holy Spirit and
*   the Virgin Mary*
*   and was made man.*
For our sake he was crucified under
*   Pontius Pilate;*
he suffered death and was buried.
On the third day he rose again
*   in accordance with the Scriptures;*
he ascended into heaven
and is seated at the right hand
*   of the Father.*
He will come again in glory to judge
*   the living and the dead,*
and his kingdom will have no end.
We believe in the Holy Spirit,
the Lord, the giver of life,
who proceeds from the Father and
*   the Son,*
with the Father and the Son he is
*   worshipped and glorified.*
He has spoken through the prophets.

'The Creed does not say what someone else believes but what I (or we) believe... it is not only the story of the world, but it is also autobiographical in character. It is profoundly personal testimony, or it is misused.'
Nicholas Lash, theologian

'God was reconciling the world to himself in Christ, not counting men's sins against them.'

Paul, 2 Corinthians 5:19

✳

According to Christianity, Jesus died for the sins of the world.

'*We believe in one holy, catholic and apostolic Church.*
We acknowledge one baptism for the forgiveness of sins.
We look for the resurrection of the dead,
and the life of the world to come.
Amen.'

KEY BELIEFS

† Christians worship one God in a Trinity: Father, Son and Holy Spirit.
† The persons of the Trinity are coequal and are all part of God.
† Jesus is God made man, the 'Son' who truly took flesh.
† Jesus died for all when Pilate was governor, that is, in real history. He is not a myth.
† Jesus rose again on the third day, alive spiritually and powerfully.
† The Holy Spirit lives in believers, makes them holy and speaks through the prophets today.
† The people form a church, an assembly, that is worldwide ('catholic') and based upon the teaching of the apostles ('apostolic').
† Forgiveness of sins is freely offered.
† There is life after death, the resurrection of the body.

ATONEMENT

The death of Jesus is seen to have saving significance. This is the atonement, the 'covering' for sin, reconciliation – the bringing of people back into a right relationship with God. There are many models of the atonement in the Bible. One key picture found in the Old Testament is that of sacrifice. The Jews had to offer various sacrifices in the Temple, as the shedding of blood secured their forgiveness for a limited period. Christians believe that the blood of Jesus shed on the cross secures peace and forgiveness forever. God himself took human form and offered himself in perfect sacrifice. God's action is sometimes depicted as that of a judge who, having pronounced sentence, steps into the dock to take the punishment himself, such is his love for the accused.

CHURCH

'Church' translates from the Greek word *ekklesia* in the New Testament. This means an assembly, all those called to follow Jesus who gather in worship. Paul also calls the church the 'body of Christ'. The church is not the building but the people.

Sadly, however, Christians have fought and disagreed, splitting into various groups (denominations) over the centuries. An early major split occurred in 1054 when the Western church split from the Eastern church. A later split took place at the Reformation in the sixteenth century, when a number of Reformers or Protestants sought to change the church by returning to what they believed were its original and pure teachings.

Paths to Peace

'Be still, and know that I am God.'
Psalm 46:10

CHRISTIAN PRAYER

Christian prayer is made to God the Father, through the Son, and in the power of the Holy Spirit. Prayer is trinitarian. Prayer becomes a cooperation, a partnership.

Christians seek to come into the presence of God, praising and exalting his name. Believers have the conviction that they have the right to come before God because Jesus has made them acceptable; his blood has atoned for sin and 'covers' them.

Silence

Silence and listening are as much a part of Christian prayer as any amount of words, actions or music. In a busy, media-saturated society it is hard enough to be still and to listen to oneself, let alone to hear the voice of God or to sense his presence. Adoration prayers worship the presence of God, saying nothing or very little. When humans are in the presence of one whom they love, it is good to be with them, to touch them, to look into their eyes. Words are almost superfluous. Thérèse of Lisieux used to slip into her convent chapel to kneel before God. She said, 'He looks at me and I look at him.'

THE LORD'S PRAYER

When Jesus' disciples asked him to teach them how to pray, he taught them the 'Our Father':

Our Father, who art in heaven,
hallowed be thy name;
thy kingdom come;
thy will be done,
on earth as it is in heaven.
Give us this day our daily bread.
And forgive us our trespasses,
as we forgive those who trespass
against us.
And lead us not into temptation;
but deliver us from evil.
For thine is the kingdom,
the power, and the glory
for ever and ever.
Amen.

'In the same way the Spirit helps us in our weakness. We do not know what we ought to pray for, but the Spirit himself intercedes for us with groans that words cannot express.'
Paul, Romans 8:26

'Prayer is like throwing a stick in a river as lots of other people throw in their sticks. They all flow along. The river is the Holy Spirit.'
Fr Basil,
a Russian Orthodox priest

✳

This prayer of Jesus focuses on three basic elements: God as Father, the coming kingdom and forgiveness:

† 'Father' – The Christian's main name for God is 'Father'. God's names in the Old Testament could be many and varied – from Lord to King to Most High to cite but a few. Jesus gave the most honour to an intimate title.

† Kingdom – Jesus taught his disciples to pray for the kingdom to come, for God's rule or way. The kingdom can come in partial ways too, when a difficult or unjust situation changes, or a person finds forgiveness and healing.

† Forgiveness – Jesus taught that forgiveness is conditional upon our forgiveness. If we refuse to forgive others, it sets up a spiritual short-circuit. We will be judged as we judge others. The Lord's Prayer shows a structure of praise, petition and confession, returning at the end to praise.

CONVERSION – 'BEING SAVED'

Many people are either not brought up in the Christian faith, or they are believers in name only. If, in later life, they hear about Jesus and are convinced in their hearts that he is the Son of God, then they make a commitment to him. They accept him as their personal Lord and Saviour. This could be the result of a period of heart-searching and reading, or conversing with committed Christians. It could be after attending a study course for open-minded seekers such as the Alpha Course, which is becoming very popular in the West. Here, people gather for a meal and then listen to a series of talks about the basics of the Christian faith. It might also be the result of

attending a large convention hosted by an evangelist. They might then respond to an invitation to give their lives to Christ. They will be called to pray with someone and say words such as:

'Lord Jesus, I turn to you.
I confess that I am a sinner and
that you died for me.
I thank you and ask you to forgive
me and come into my life. Amen.'

This is called 'being saved' or becoming 'born again'.

RIGHT LIVING

Jesus taught many virtues and ways of life. The key was to respect others as yourself. He was concerned to look at the motives of the heart and not just ritual or external actions. Some key and challenging elements of his ethical teaching can be found in the Sermon on the Mount in Matthew 5–7. The section printed below is known as the Beatitudes:

'Now when he saw the crowds, he went
up on a mountainside and sat down.
His disciples came to him, and he
began to teach them saying:

"Blessed are the poor in spirit, for
theirs is the kingdom of heaven.
Blessed are those who mourn,
for they will be comforted.
Blessed are the meek,
for they will inherit the earth.
Blessed are those who hunger and
thirst for righteousness,
for they will be filled.
Blessed are the merciful,
for they will be shown mercy.

Famous Christians working for justice

Christians who seek to live out the values of Christ make an impact upon those around them. 'Salvation' is not just a personal, spiritual matter, but it involves mending relationships between people and seeking justice in society.

For example, Martin Luther King (1929–68) was a black Baptist minister in Atlanta, Georgia, in the USA. He became a leader in the civil rights movement in the 1950s and 1960s. He helped to organize peaceful protests, including a march on Washington of 250,000 people in 1962. He was fighting against racist laws and attitudes where blacks and whites were not free to eat together in restaurants or go to school together. He was shot by an assassin in April 1968.

Mother Teresa (1910–97) ran a group of Roman Catholic nuns, the Missionaries of Charity, in Calcutta, India. They lived in a room next to a Hindu temple, which they called *Nirmal Hriday*, 'Place of the Pure Heart'. She took in sick and dying people from the streets where they had been abandoned. They were fed and cared for, and the terminally ill would die in arms of love.

Once, she found a boy who had been dumped in a rubbish heap. He was taken back and nursed into health. Early in her work, some locals threw stones at her and feared that she was only there to try to convert them. A Hindu priest watched her carrying the dying inside and stopped the people. 'This is a living god, and not one made of stone, that is walking among us!' he said.

Both these believers show certain Christian beliefs and values in action. Human beings, no matter what race, or how rich or poor, are all made in the 'image of God'.

'So in everything, do to others what you would have them do to you, for this sums up the Law and the Prophets.'
Jesus, Matthew 7:12

✳

Mother Teresa blesses a child in India.

Blessed are the pure in heart,
for they will see God.
Blessed are the peacemakers,
for they will be called sons of God.
Blessed are those who are persecuted
because of righteousness,
for theirs is the kingdom of heaven.
Blessed are you when people insult you,
persecute you and falsely say all
kinds of evil against you because
of me.
Rejoice and be glad, because great is
your reward in heaven,
for in the same way they persecuted
the prophets who were before you.'"

Jesus, Matthew 5:1–12

A pilgrim prays at the Holy Sepulchre – the traditional site of the burial of Christ.

Awe and Wonder

'Holy, holy, holy
is the Lord God Almighty,
who was, and is, and is to come.'

Revelation 4:8

THE HOLY ONE

Christian worship seeks to be in the presence of the living God. In both the Old Testament and the New Testament, the song of the angels in heaven is 'Holy, holy, holy…'. These words are sung or recited in Christian worship in the communion service, reminding the earthly worshippers that they are standing before heaven and before all

Gifts of the Spirit

The New Testament states that the Holy Spirit will help people to live the Christian life, to pray and to worship. The Spirit is said to bring a number of supernatural gifts that can be a sign of his presence. The most renowned of these is 'speaking in tongues' and it can be the cause of great misunderstanding. The gift of 'tongues' is said to be the ability to praise God in a language that you have never learned. This might be an ancient or a living language, or that of the angels. People who claim this gift say it is uplifting and soothing, and is a good way of praying when they do not know how to pray for someone.

Some Christians will also sing together in harmony using tongues, a phenomenon noted in the early church and referred to by Augustine of Hippo as 'jubilation', a joyful singing without words. Paul describes some of the gifts of the Spirit as follows:

'There are different kinds of gifts, but the same Spirit. There are different kinds of service, but the same Lord. There are different kinds of working, but the same God works all of them in all men.

'Now to each one the manifestation of the Spirit is given for the common good. To one there is given through the Spirit the message of wisdom, to another the message of knowledge by means of the same Spirit, to another faith by the same Spirit, to another gifts of healing by that one Spirit, to another miraculous powers, to another prophecy, to another distinguishing between spirits, to another speaking in different kinds of tongues, and to still another the interpretation of tongues. All these are the work of one and the same Spirit, and he gives them to each one, just as he determines.'

1 Corinthians 12:4–11

Christians expect to be guided by God and to have a sense of his presence among them.

the angels. The Christian is declared to be part of a priesthood of all believers, all of whom can equally offer praise to God through Jesus.

Christian worship can involve movement, music and song, words, symbols and silence.

EARLY CHRISTIAN WORSHIP

The first Christians adapted the Jewish synagogue services: singing praises and psalms, reading the Scriptures and then having a time of instruction. Following on from this would have been the celebration of holy communion, the sharing of bread and wine. The first Christians would have stood to pray, lifting their hands in worship. This was the common pattern in the ancient world, for pagan worship too. Seats and pews were only introduced into some churches much, much later on. To this day, Eastern churches have few seats and people may have to stand for hours. The practice of raising hands in worship has been rediscovered by some in modern times.

MOVEMENT

Some Christians are taught specific body movements to help them worship. They might kneel, to show humility. They might make the sign of the cross over their heads and chests – and there are different ways of doing this in the East and the West!

They might raise their hands, as mentioned above, or open their hands, symbolizing their willingness to be open before God.

In some Eastern churches, believers will bow low and prostrate themselves fully before God, acknowledging his majesty.

MUSIC

Christian music has adopted many different styles through the ages. The musical worship of the early church would have been akin to that of the Jerusalem Temple where various chants and instruments could be used. The Eastern churches shun the use of instruments, using only the melodies of the human voice. Western monastic music centred on the unaccompanied voice in chant and plainsong. Parish churches would have various instruments too, whether wind or string. There were no organs until recent centuries.

The victorious lamb of God is a symbol of the sacrifice and resurrection of Jesus.

Spiritual renewal movements produce new songs and styles of music. The Wesley brothers composed a new set of hymns during the eighteenth century, and many came from groups like the Salvation Army in the nineteenth century. Modern renewal movements tend to produce shorter songs, choruses and chants that are designed to be repeated several times. These are often based upon verses of Scripture:

> 'God is spirit, and his worshippers must worship in spirit and in truth'
>
> Jesus, John 4:24

Journey into Mystery

> 'Now we see but a poor reflection as in a mirror; then we shall see face to face. Now I know in part; then I shall know fully...'
>
> Paul, 1 Corinthians 13:12

PICTURES OF THE INVISIBLE

Christianity has a number of symbols that it uses in its worship and decorations. These can suggest deep mysteries of the faith. Words, actions and symbols are all imperfect ways of capturing and expressing the mystery of God and the drama of salvation. The great medieval theologian, Thomas Aquinas, said that they were just 'adequate' for the task, but there is so much that cannot be said, that we do not understand.

The cross This simple object masks depths of spirituality and theology. For Christians it is not just an instrument of

 Holy communion

This is a sharing of bread and wine after the Last Supper of Jesus. A thanksgiving prayer is said over the bread and wine and the Holy Spirit is called down upon them and the worshippers. The words of Jesus at the Last Supper are also repeated, 'This is my body... This is my blood.'

The communion (also called the eucharist, the mass and the Lord's Supper) is a beautiful sacrament of sharing and belonging to a family. It is also a proclamation of the death and resurrection of Jesus, a potent reminder of his sacrifice. Christians differ in their understanding of exactly how the bread and wine 'are' the body and blood of Christ. For some this is merely a symbol; for others, such as Roman Catholics, it is a substantial reality; others, again, accept that Jesus is there when the elements are blessed but refuse to define how. The interpretations are many and varied.

torture and execution, but a symbol of redemption. Jesus died to bring forgiveness and atonement. Many are the theories of how this was achieved, from blood sacrifice, to an example of love, to victory over evil. At heart, it is a mystery.

The lamb The lamb symbol shows an animal that was slain and still bears the wound. It is alive, holding a flag of victory. Jesus is the lamb who was slain in the New Testament, another reference to the mystery of his atoning death, but also to the wonder of his resurrection.

The dove The Holy Spirit is symbolized

> 'I sensed a Presence, a Spirit, as people gathered to worship. There was something there.'
>
> Mark, an agnostic visitor to a church worship service in Ghana

✳

as a dove descending from heaven in the Gospels. It is in this way that Jesus experienced the Spirit at his baptism. The dove suggests hope and peace, a gentle presence of love. The Spirit has another side, depicted as wind, water and fire, suggesting cleansing action.

DOORS TO HEAVEN

Christianity has a number of special rituals called 'sacraments'. These are actions that convey a spiritual blessing. Some churches have seven sacraments, others only two. The number depends upon how a sacrament is defined. If it is seen as something that was directly instituted by Jesus, then this applies only to baptism and holy communion. If it refers to a practice of the early church, then confirmation (or chrismation), ordination, marriage, confession and anointing of the sick can be added. Behind the idea of a sacrament is the affirmation that God can bless material things; bread and wine can convey the divine.

BAPTISM

'Baptism' comes from a Greek word meaning to be submerged. Going under the water suggests dying to an old life and rising to a new one. The water also suggests washing. Some Christians practise total immersion, putting a candidate right under the water in a pool or large tank; others pour water over the candidate's head. To follow Jesus involves a turning away from an old life and a renewal of the spirit; a second birth, as Jesus said: 'I tell you the truth, no one can see the kingdom of God unless he is born again' (John 3:3).

Resurrection

The Jews came to believe in a general resurrection of the dead. This belief was widespread among them at the time of Jesus, though not universally held. Jesus had stepped into this new life before anyone else, according to the first Christians. Thus he became known as 'the firstborn from the dead' ('He is the beginning and the firstborn from among the dead, so that in everything he might have the supremacy.' (Colossians 1:18).

According to the Bible, Jesus made several resurrection appearances to his disciples, including one occasion on which 'he appeared to more than five hundred of the brothers at the same time' (1 Corinthians 15:6). The resurrection of Jesus is central to the Christian faith as it confirmed that Jesus was the Son of God and that he had defeated death. Indeed, the apostle Paul went as far as to claim that if Jesus had not been raised from the dead, 'your faith is futile; you are still in your sins' (1 Corinthians 15:17).

HANDS AND OIL

A biblical practice was to lay hands upon a person to pronounce a blessing. This happens at ordination when someone becomes a priest or a minister, and at confirmation. Confirmation is used in many churches that baptize babies. It is a ceremony that gives a young person or adult a chance to speak for themselves and make promises personally.

Hands are also used in blessing for the sick during prayer ministry. Holy oil – blessed olive oil – is also used during prayer for the sick. The idea is that this symbolizes the Holy Spirit, and olive oil was also used medicinally in the ancient world.

WINDOWS INTO HEAVEN

Orthodox Christians use sacred paintings of Christ and the saints, called icons. These are prepared with much prayer and fasting, being finally blessed by a priest. They are visual aids, but also a way of catching a glimpse of the invisible, a little window into heaven, although in symbolic form.

Making Merry

'Finally, my brothers, rejoice in the Lord!'
Paul, Philippians 3:1

Christians celebrate a number of festivals. The main ones are Christmas, Easter and Pentecost.

CHRISTMAS

This celebrates the birth of Jesus and is also known as the nativity. It was celebrated fairly late in the history of the church, after the faith became accepted by the Roman empire in the fourth century CE. The nativity adapted a pagan celebration of the sun god, Saturnalia. Jesus was not born on 25 December. It is just his official birthday; in reality, he may have been born in February or early March, or even in midsummer.

Christmas is a festival of light. Golden cloths and robes are used in many churches, with blazing candles and joyful songs. Some of the traditional Christmas carols contain deep truths about the faith. These celebrate God becoming man, the incarnation.

'One is not born a Christian; you become one.'
Tertullian, 2nd–3rd century CE North African Christian writer

'Is any one of you sick? He should call the elders of the church to pray over him and anoint him with oil in the name of the Lord.'
James 5:14

✳

A Christmas nativity scene from Mexico, arranged around the figure of the infant Christ.

EASTER

Easter, or *Pascha* in the Hebrew, is about the resurrection of Jesus. Holy Week lies before Easter Sunday, with Good Friday marking the day that Jesus died. It is called 'good', even though it was a sad event, because Christians believe that Jesus died to save humanity. At Easter, there are many different customs around the world, but lighted candles are often held aloft by the congregations, who shout 'Christ is risen! He is risen indeed!'

Saints' days

Many Christians celebrate saints' days. In the New Testament all believers are called 'saints', meaning those called and set apart.

Outstanding men and women are called 'Saints' by many believers. Reformed Churches hesitate to do this as they stress that all are saints, although we are far from perfect; perfection only comes when we enter heaven. All can look up to heroes of the faith, though, in their own way. The Virgin Mary is given special honour by many because she gave birth to Jesus.

Pentecostal believers at worship.

PENTECOST

This celebrates the gift of the Holy Spirit to the church, recalling the first disciples on the day of Pentecost (which is also a Jewish festival, about the giving of the *Torah* to Moses). The Bible describes this with symbols of rushing wind and tongues of fire:

> *'When the day of Pentecost came, they were all together in one place. Suddenly a sound like the blowing of a violent wind came from heaven and filled the whole house where they were sitting. They saw what seemed to be tongues of fire that separated and came to rest on each of them. All of them were filled with the Holy Spirit and began to speak in other tongues as the Spirit enabled them.'*
>
> Acts 2:1–4

PILGRIMAGE

There are special places for Christians, associated with events in the life of Jesus or the saints. Thus Jerusalem has always been a special place of pilgrimage, the city where Jesus preached, was crucified and rose again. Rome, too, is special to Roman Catholics, as this is the site of the apostle Peter's martyrdom and burial, and the residence of his successors, the Popes. Pilgrimage began with gatherings around the tombs of early martyrs as prayers were said and communion was shared. When the Roman empire began to tolerate Christianity, pilgrims journeyed to the Holy Land and walked along the Via Dolorosa, the road that Jesus walked to the cross. They also prayed, as they do today, in the Church of the Holy Sepulchre, the traditional site of the tomb where Jesus' body was placed.

Roman Catholics believe that the Virgin Mary has appeared at various times in various places, urging people to come and pray in those sacred spots where they will find healing power. Lourdes, in southern France, is one such place. The Virgin is said to have appeared to St Bernardette in 1858 when she was a girl of only 14.

Pilgrimages are adventures involving a journey. God is everywhere, but some places are felt to be specially blessed, and many have prayed there for years. There, people claim to find relief from worry, sometimes an easing of pain or an inner strength that they did not have before. There can be a party spirit, a sense of celebration and joy as well as serious moments and times of quiet reflection.

Today

> *'Jesus Christ is the same yesterday, today and for ever.'*
>
> Hebrews 13:8

UNITY

The greatest problem facing the Christian church today is division. What began as a unified spiritual movement with a strong sense of 'family' has split over the centuries into a number of denominations. Human nature being what it is, there were bound to be disputes. Politics and power also came into play. As soon as Emperor Constantine accepted Christianity as the official religion of the Roman Empire in the fourth century CE, compromise and status came into play. A major division occurred between East and West in 1054, and the Western church itself divided during the Reformation in the sixteenth century.

> 'I felt nothing special. People were coming and going, stopping in silence. Then I noticed an elderly woman kneeling, touching the place where Jesus' body had lain. She was weeping silently. Then I started to wipe the tears from my eyes. That moved me. I had come all this way, and it took another believer to move me to pray.'
>
> Mark, a pilgrim at the Church of the Holy Sepulchre

> 'I went to Lourdes hoping. I was afraid that I might go blind. I came back, touched by God. My eyes were no different, but I no longer had any fear.'
>
> Ewa, a Polish pilgrim at Lourdes

✳

'May they be brought to complete unity to let the world know that you sent me and have loved them even as you have loved me.'
Prayer of Jesus in John 17:23

'Paul tells us that "in Christ, there is neither male nor female" (Galatians 3:28). I can stand as equal to any male believer before God, and I am overjoyed to share in the priestly ministry.'
Francesca, Anglican woman priest

Renewal and church growth

Sporadically, throughout the history of the church, the signs, wonders and experiences mentioned in the pages of the New Testament have occurred. There have been visions, healings, speaking in tongues and words of prophecy. However, these became more evident in churches in the twentieth century than at any other time since the early centuries of the church. A revival of these gifts and the sense of a personal blessing of the Holy Spirit began in the early 1900s and spread to other groups. The 1960s and 1970s saw such renewal experiences coming into the mainstream churches such as the Roman Catholic Church and the Anglican church. Charismatic or Pentecostal style Christian groups are the fastest growing in the early twenty-first century. More significantly, the areas in which the church is growing most quickly in this way are to be found in the developing world. Although churches in the West struggle to attract members, Latin America, Africa and areas of the Far East have seen phenomenal church growth. Their services might last for several hours, but the people think nothing of this. Seoul, in Korea, has a mega-church of thousands, and Brazilian and African missionaries are coming to Europe to evangelize the lands that once evangelized them. These lands tend to be less materialistic and more open to the spiritual and to relationships.

Particular branches of the church might be the established or dominant group in a nation, such as the Church of England, and others have been persecuted or restricted in their freedom to worship. This led to struggles and migrations, such as the Pilgrim Fathers leaving England for North America.

Sometimes, blood has been shed in the name of Christ (and the security of the state) as Catholics burned Protestants as heretics, and Protestants executed Catholics as traitors. This is a horrendous scandal and a blot on the face of Christianity.

The twentieth century saw major attempts to draw the churches together in Europe. The experience of two catastrophic World Wars helped this impetus, and the World Council of Churches was set up in 1948. The idea was that there would be no lasting peace in Europe if there were no peace between the churches.

Until the 1960s, Roman Catholics were very restricted if they wished to worship with other Christians. Many of these limitations were removed with the reforms of the Second Vatican Council, and ecumenism was firmly promoted. The term 'ecumenical' comes from the Greek word *oikoumenos*, meaning 'the inhabited world'. Christians lived in 'one world' and should get on together. Working in unity is also a good witness to outsiders and non-believers. There are still issues and disagreements but a greater trust and closeness of heart.

LIBERTY
Parts of the developing world, such as Latin America, have developed a system of prayer, worship and political protest.

This is known as 'liberation theology', and it is widespread in the Roman Catholic Church in those areas. Local people meet together in supportive, prayerful communities led by nuns, lay leaders or priests. They praise God, share communion, read the Bible and then apply what they hear to the problems around them, such as providing better resources for a school or clearing drains.

ETHICS

There are debates about traditional Christian values and modern society. The role of women in the church has been a major issue. In the past, they were excluded from leadership (apart from Mother Superiors in convents). There have been holy and active women saints through the ages, but they have not usually taught, and they have not celebrated the sacraments. A number of churches have admitted women to ministry in the twentieth and twenty-first centuries. The Orthodox and Roman Catholic Churches have resisted this move, arguing that it is against the tradition of the church. Both communions are looking at how to affirm women as much as possible, without ordaining them as priests.

CHRISTIANITY   at a glance...

- ◆ When did it begin? – The early part of the first century CE.
- ◆ The founder – Jesus of Nazareth (c. 4 BCE – 33 CE).
- ◆ God – God as Trinity, that is, three persons in one, Father, Son and Holy Spirit. Invisible, transcendent but also active in the world.
- ◆ Redeemer figure – Jesus is seen as the redeemer of humanity. He is believed to be God made man, and his death on the cross has brought forgiveness and the possibility of a relationship with God. Forgiveness cannot be earned; God moved towards humanity first, dying on the cross and offering to bless us.
- ◆ Scriptures – Christians use the Hebrew Scriptures, the Old Testament, and the New Testament. This contains 27 books, made up of four Gospels about Jesus, 21 letters, one book about the first Christians and one book of prophecy.
- ◆ Beliefs – God as Trinity; Jesus as God incarnate; Jesus died for humankind; Jesus rose from the dead in a new, spiritual body; the Holy Spirit can live inside believers.
- ◆ Place of worship – The church is the people assembled together; church buildings can be simple and plain, or very ornate. These will often contain a table or an altar for sharing holy communion and a place for reading the Bible and preaching.
- ◆ Sacred food – Bread and wine are taken, blessed and shared out in memory of Jesus at the Last Supper. The bread is a sign of his body, the wine a sign of his blood.
- ◆ Main festivals – Christmas celebrates the birth of Jesus; Easter recalls his death and resurrection; Pentecost remembers the descent of the Holy Spirit.
- ◆ Key Symbols – the cross; fire, water and a dove for the Holy Spirit.

Islam

*'In the Name of God, the Merciful, the Compassionate.
Praise belongs to God, the Lord of all Being...'*

The Qur'an, *Sura* 1:1–2

The faith of Islam is claimed by Muslims as the original, revealed faith. They believe it was revealed to Adam and the prophets, including Abraham, Moses, David and Jesus. Afterwards, in the early seventh century CE, a new prophet, Muhammad, burst upon the scene in Arabia, confirming the earlier revelations. His prophetic utterances were learned by heart and were later collected into the Qur'an.

ISLAM AND ALLAH

The word 'Islam' comes from the root verb *slm* in Arabic, meaning peace or submission. It has a double meaning, and Muslims believe that they should submit to the will of God (Allah) and thus find peace. A Muslim is one who submits, from the same root verb in Arabic.

The first *Sura* (section) of the Qur'an, the *Fattiha* prayer, speaks of this submission and path to peace:

> 'In the Name of God, the Merciful,
>   the Compassionate.
> Praise belongs to God, the Lord of all
>   Being,
> the All-merciful, the All-compassionate
> the Master of the Day of Doom.
> Thee only we serve; to Thee alone we
>   pray for succour.
> Guide us in the straight path,
> the path of those whom Thou hast blessed,
> Not of those against whom Thou art
>   wrathful,
> nor of those who are astray.'

The word 'Allah' is Arabic for God. It now means 'the God' or 'the one God'. The Arabian tribes had previously worshipped many gods, with a pantheon headed by Allah as chief deity, along with his female consort, Allat, and his three daughters.

Muhammad heard of the one God of the Jews and the Christians on his travels, and identified Allah as the same, 'the one God', rejecting worship of his consorts and rejecting the idea that he could have any offspring.

THE LAND

Arabia was a collection of self-governing tribes who were ruled by powerful families. The land nestled between empires – that of the Byzantine Christians to the west and to the north, and that of the Persians to the east. A series of trade routes lay across the peninsula and passed through Makkah, making it a prosperous trading post. To add to Makkah's fortunes was the existence of an ancient structure, the *Ka'aba*. This was a cube-shaped building that housed many images of deities. Set in its foundations was the black stone, said to have fallen from heaven. This was probably a meteorite, and the pagan tribes had sacrificed animals on this for generations, staining it black. The tribes performed an annual pilgrimage, circling around it to ensure fertility.

Muhammad transformed the use of the *Ka'aba* and the pilgrimage. In Muslim belief it was the first house of God built by Adam, and later restored by Abraham. The stone was the sacred stone upon which Abraham nearly sacrificed his son, Ishmael.

In a nutshell

Muhammad was based at Makkah (known in the West as Mecca), a central trading city in Arabia at that time. At first, he and his followers were insulted and persecuted. They fled to Medina, and after a series of battles, Muhammad took control of the Arabian tribes. He may have had no intention to push any further, believing that he was a prophet to the Arabs, but after his death, his successors gained lands in the Persian empire and the Byzantine Roman empire. They went into Syria, North Africa and the Persian Gulf. Islam had become a world faith and a political force to be reckoned with.

Muhammad's cave on Mount Hira, where Muhammad is said to have received a revelation from God.

The genius

Islam is a profound but simple faith. It has a clear and uncomplicated message that there is one God, the Creator, and his will is revealed by his prophets, supremely in the Qur'an.

There are prescribed rituals for daily prayer and worship and other obligations laid upon the believer. There is no Redeemer figure; Muhammad claimed to be nothing but a messenger. Jesus is honoured by Muslims, but only as a prophet.

The symbol

There are no symbols of God. The five-pointed star represents the five pillars of the Muslim faith; the moon suggests God's creation, and the new star rising over the fading moon suggests the rise of Islam.

First Steps

> 'Read, in the name of your Lord, Who
> created;
> He created man from a clot.
> Read, by your Most Generous Lord,
> Who taught by the pen,
> Who taught man what he did
>   not know.'
>
> *Sura 96:1–5*

TRADER AND SEEKER

Muhammad had been orphaned as a young boy. He was raised in Makkah by his uncle, Abu Talib, a powerful and influential man in the Quraysh tribe. Muhammad spent a good half of his life, from 582 to 610 CE, as a trader in the camel caravans dealing in livestock, leather goods and incense from the

The Revelation

Muhammad was on Mount Hira on the seventeenth night of Ramadan in 610 CE. There he experienced a vision which he came to believe was the angel Gabriel. The angel gripped him and he dared not move. He heard the command, 'Recite!' Muhammad was illiterate, but the first sentence of the Qu'ran came from his lips.

There was a period of fear and scepticism – what had seized him? A desert spirit (*jinn*)? Was he like one of the possessed *shaman* or healers that the tribes produced? He saw another vision of the angel, huge, towering to the sky. He went home, shaking, to Khadija, who sought the advice of the *hanif* Waraqa. He sensed that this was the calling to be a prophet.

It was to be two years before another revelation, and this time it was longer, and in the daylight. Muhammad was often left exhausted, shivering with cold, and covered with a blanket. He felt weighed down, and he would slump with his head between his knees when a revelation came to him. He said it was like a bell being struck.

Yemen. Muhammad's journeys would have taken him to Egypt, Syria and Persia. The journey to Syria passed many ancient ruins such as the hidden city of Petra and sites of biblical stories. The central spring at Petra was regarded as the spring opened by Moses and is known as *Ain Musa* to this day. In 595 CE Muhammad was employed by an older woman, a distant cousin, Khadija. They were soon married. She was impressed by his good reputation and by stories that he was recognized by monks as a holy man. (There are various stories about this, such as the monk Bahira seeing the mark of a prophet upon him as a young boy.)

THE SEEKER

Muhammad became one of the *hanifs*, a group of seekers around Makkah. They knew the stories of the Bible. They believed that Abraham had walked their land and had dedicated Arabia to the one God, the God of the Jews and the Christians. They called him 'Allah' after their chief deity. There were different Christian groups around, such as the persecuted Nestorians, or the Coptic believers from Egypt and Abyssinia. There were settlements of Jewish traders, and Zoroastrians with their own version of monotheism from Persia. We know of four outstanding *hanifs* who were contemporaries of Muhammad. Three eventually embraced forms of Christianity; one, Zayd, wandered as an exile from Makkah, seeking truth from many teachers. Zayd returned when he heard that a new prophet was in Makkah, but he was killed along the way.

Muhammad knew the Old Testament stories and heard parts of the Gospels. He would have seen Christian monks at prayer (there was a chain of monasteries down the eastern coast of Arabia). He began to withdraw to a cave on Mount Hira for quiet meditation.

The mosque in Medina.

THE PROPHET

In 615 CE, Muhammad felt called to preach publicly. He gained a small group of converts in Makkah at first, but the tribal leaders mocked and persecuted them, fearing that the attack on idols and pagan gods would lose them trade and would threaten the pilgrimage season. Some of the Muslims fled to the Christian kingdom of Abyssinia for protection, and the group finally settled at the oasis of Yathrib (now Madina).

Muhammad joined them on 15 June 622 CE. This was the start of the Hegira, the Muslim era, and their calendar dates from this time.

A series of battles followed as the Muslim community defended itself from hostile tribes and some Jewish communities. In 632 CE, Muhammad took control of Makkah. Later that year, Muhammad died from a fever. His close friend and companion, Abu Bakr, was acclaimed as Muhammad's successor. Muhammad had commanded and fought in numerous battles towards the end of his life.

The whole of Arabia was united under Islam. Later, division came into the community over rival claimants for the role of Caliph or Khalifah ('Successor'). The majority formed *Sunni* Islam and others formed *Shi'a* Islam.

> 'Never once did I receive a revelation
> without thinking my soul had been
> torn away from me.'
>
> Muhammad

An-Nur – The Light

God is never depicted pictorially – Muslims forbid any images that might become idols. God is mysterious and beyond form. One *Sura* of the Qu'ran compares God to light:

> 'God is the Light of the heavens
> and the earth;
> the likeness of His Light is as a niche
> wherein is a lamp
> (the lamp is a glass, the glass as it were
> of a glittering star)
> kindled from a Blessed Tree,
> an olive that is neither of the East
> or of the West
> whose oil well nigh would shine,
> even if no fire touched it;
> Light upon Light;
> (God guides to His Light whom He will).'
>
> **Sura** 24:35–37

The Goal

> 'Praise be to Allah, the Lord of the
> worlds...'
>
> *Sura* 1:2

ONE GOD

Allah is simply 'God' for Arabic speakers, using the Arabic word for 'the one God'. It is linked to the same Semitic word as 'El', one of the Old Testament names for God.

God's nature is summed up in the *Bismillah*, a prayer that opens each *Sura* of the Qu'ran, and which is prayed by devout Muslims throughout the day. It opens their prayer times and blesses their food.

The words for 'compassionate' and 'merciful', *rahman* and *rahim*, are linked to the Semitic word for 'womb'.

God is holy and transcendent, but also merciful. In his mercy, he sent down the Qur'an for our guidance, so Muslims believe. He has not stayed aloof and in heaven, but sends his messengers to draw humanity back to him.

GOD IS NEAR

God is also immanent, close to his creation. *Sura* 57:3 declares:

'He is the First and the Last, the Outer and the Inner, and He has knowledge of everything.'

God is seen to be close to people and to love them:

'Say, "If you love God, follow me; then God will love you and forgive your sins." God is Forgiving, Merciful.'

Sura 3:31

'We have indeed created man, and we know what his soul insinuates to him. We are to him closer than the jugular vein.'

Sura 50:16

✳

A Muslim boy cups his hands and says his own, personal prayers.

The 99 Beautiful Names

Muslims have drawn up a list of the 99 names of God as revealed in the Qu'ran. These are attributes, titles and descriptions of his nature and activity:

Ar-Rahman, the Compassionate
Ar-Rahim, the Merciful
Al-Malik, the Sovereign Lord
Al-Quddus, the Holy
As-Salam, the Source of Peace
Al-Mu'min, the Guardian of Faith
Al-Muhaymin, the Protector
Al-Aziz, the Mighty
Al-Jabbar, the Compeller
Al-Mutakabbir, the Majestic
Al-Khaliq, the Creator
Al-Bari, the Evolver
Al-Musawwir, the Fashioner
Al-Ghaffar, the Forgiver
Al-Qahhar, the Subduer
Al-Wahhab, the Bestower
Ar-Razzaq, the Provider
Al-Fattah, the Opener
Al-'Alim, the All-Knowing
Al-Qabi, the Constrictor
Al-Basit, the Expander
Al-Khafid, the Abaser
Ar-Rafi, the Exalter
Al-Mu'izz, the Honourer
Al-Muzill, the Dishonourer
As-Sami, the All-Hearing
Al-Basir, the All-Seeing
Al-Hakam, the Judge
Al-'Adl, the Just
Al-Latif, the Subtle One
Al-Khabir, the Aware
Al-Halim, the Forbearing One

Al-Azim, the Great One
Al-Ghafur, the All-Forgiving
Ash-Shakur, the Appreciative
Al-Ali, the Most High
Al-Kabir, the Most Great
Al-Hafiz, the Preserver
Al-Muqit, the Maintainer
Al-Hasib, the Reckoner
Al-Jalil, the Sublime One
Al-Karim, the Generous One
Ar-Raqib, the Watchful
Al-Mujib, the Responsive
Al-Wasi, the All-Embracing
Al-Hakim, the Wise
Al-Wadud, the Loving
Al-Majid, the Most Glorious One
Al-Ba'ith, the Resurrector
Ash-Shahid, the Witness
Al-Haqq, the Truth
Al-Wakil, the Trustee
Al-Qawi, the Most Strong
Al-Matin, the Firm One
Al-Wali, the Protective Friend
Al-Hamid, the Praiseworthy
Al-Muhsi, the Reckoner
Al-Mubdi, the Originator
Al-Mu'id, the Restorer
Al-Muhyi, the Giver of Life
Al-Mumit, the Creator of Death
Al-Hayy, the Alive
Al-Qayyum, the Self-Subsisting
Al-Wajid, the Finder
Al-Majid, the Noble
Al-Wahid, the Unique
Al-Ahad, the One
As-Samad, the Eternal

Al-Qadir, the Able
Al-Muqradir, the Powerful
Al-Muqaddim, the Expediter
Al-Mu'akhkhir, the Delayer
Al-Awwal, the First
Al-Akhir, the Last
Az-Zahir, the Manifest
Al-Batin, the Hidden
Al-Wali, the Governor
Al-Muta'Ali, the Most Exalted
Al-Barr, the Source of all Goodness
Al-Tawwab, the Acceptor of Repentance
Al-Munraqim, the Avenger
Al-Afuw, the Pardoner
Ar-Ra'uf, the Compassionate
Malik-ul-Mulk, the Eternal Owner of Sovereignty
Dhul-Jalal-Wal-Ikram, the Lord of Majesty and Bounty
Al-Muqsit, the Equitable
Al-Jame, the Gatherer
Al-Ghani, the Self-sufficient
Al-Mughni, the Enricher
Al-Mani, the Preventer
An-Nafi, the Propitious
Ad-Darr, the Distresser
An-Nur, the Light
Al-Hadi, the Guide
Al-Badi, the Incomparable
Al-Baqi, the Everlasting
Al-Warith, the Supreme Inheritor
At-Rashid, the Guide to the Right Path
As-Sabur, the Patient

The goal of a Muslim is to return to God, his Lord and Beloved:

> 'Did you, then, think that We created you in vain and that unto Us you will not be returned?'
>
> *Sura* 23:115

Faithful Muslims who are judged worthy will be welcomed into Paradise to live in the light and presence of God after death.

TAWHID

Tawhid is the belief that there is only one true God. God is a sublime unity and not many. Polytheism is rejected as 'idolatry', or *shirk*. The Qur'an rejects any idea that God had a female consort, as pagan Arabs taught, or that he had any offspring. There is a rejection of the deity of Christ, and of any idea of the Trinity:

> 'And when God said, "O Jesus, son of Mary, did you say to the people; 'Take me and my mother as gods, apart from God?'"
>
> *Sura* 5:116

The Qur'an is consistent that God has no equals and that he has not taken a son:

> 'And they say, "The Compassionate has taken to Himself a son." You have, indeed, made a shocking assertion...'
>
> *Sura* 19:88–89

JUDGEMENT

God is merciful, but he is also holy. Time after time, the Qur'an warns about the Day of Judgement that is to come:

> 'O believers, spend of what We have provided for you before a Day comes in which there is neither trading, nor friendship, nor intercession. The unbelievers are the wrongdoers.'
>
> *Sura* 2:254

Teachers of the Way

> 'And when a Messenger came to them from God confirming what they had, a group of those who were given the Book cast the Book of God behind their backs as if they knew nothing.'
>
> *Sura* 2:101

THE SEAL OF THE PROPHETS

Muhammad is seen as the last in a long line of prophets. He is known as 'the Seal of the Prophets' as he confirms all that has gone before him. 'Muhammad is... the Messenger of God and the seal of the Prophets...' (*Sura* 33:40).

The idea is that there will not be another prophet after him. Muhammad has revealed the accurate, correct revelation of God, which had been lost or corrupted before him. This now resides in the words of the Qur'an for all time.

Muhammad himself was just a man, a *rasul* (messenger) and a *nabi* (prophet).

All believe in God, His angels, His books and His Messengers. We make no distinction between any of His Messengers. And they say: 'We hear and obey. Grant us Your forgiveness, our Lord. And to You is our return.'
Sura 2:285

✳

'I try to read the Qur'an each night. It makes me feel really peaceful and clean.'

Fatima, a Muslim teenage girl

✳

Prophets and messengers

The Qur'an teaches that God has sent his word through various messengers throughout history, starting with the first man, Adam. The term for messenger is *rasul*, similar to the word apostle in Christianity. It is one who is sent with a message. The word for prophet is *nabi*, as in the Old Testament word for the prophets of the Jews.

Twenty-five messengers are mentioned by name in the Qur'an. The *Hadith* collections list a total of 124,000 prophets, 313 of whom were messengers. All the prophets, whether they were messengers or not, are believed to have performed miracles.

Several of the prophets mentioned in the Qur'an have counterparts in the Bible:

'And we bestowed upon [Abraham] Isaac and Jacob; each of them We guided; and Noah did We guide aforetime; and of his seed (We guided) David and Solomon and Job and Joseph and Moses and Aaron. Thus do We reward the good.'

Surah 6:84

Not all the prophets have a biblical counterpart however. For example, Hud, Salih and Luqman are all considered to be Arabian prophets.

JESUS ('ISA')

Jesus is revered by Muslims as the prophet before Muhammad. He is known in Arabic as 'Isa al-Masih', 'Jesus the Messiah'. He was born of the Virgin Mary, and he healed the sick. He is a 'word from God'. There is much here that Muslims and Christians can dialogue with, but Jesus is just a *rasul* and a *nabi*, like Muhammad:

'He [Jesus] said 'Indeed, I am the servant of God, Who gave me the Book and made me a prophet.'

Sura 19:30

Jesus' death is also a point of controversy between Christians and Muslims. The Qur'an seems to teach that Jesus was not crucified. The passage in question is in *Sura* 4:157–8:

'And their saying, "We have killed the Messiah, Jesus, son of Mary, and the Messenger of God." They have neither killed nor crucified him; but it was made to appear so unto them … rather God raised him unto Him. God is mighty and wise.'

The majority of Muslims understand this to mean that the death of Jesus was an illusion – he was really taken up to heaven. The Arabic is open to interpretation, though.

THE BOOKS

The messengers were given Books. Mention is made of the *Torah* of Moses, the Psalms of David and the Gospel of Jesus in the Qur'an. Muslims believe that these have been corrupted by the Jews and Christians, both of whom are called 'the people of the Book' in the Qur'an. The Qur'an reveals the complete message of God. There is no textual evidence that the earlier books had been changed, to be fair, but Muslims simply assume that this must have been so.

The Qur'an (meaning 'Recitation') was remembered orally in Muhammad's lifetime. The believers would learn *Suras* by heart and recite them at prayer times. Gradually, they were written down on whatever came to hand – parchment, leaves, pieces of bone. The text was written down a few years after Muhammad's death at the command of Abu Bakr and his companion, Umar. Fragments and manuscripts were collected and checked, and a definitive text was compiled.

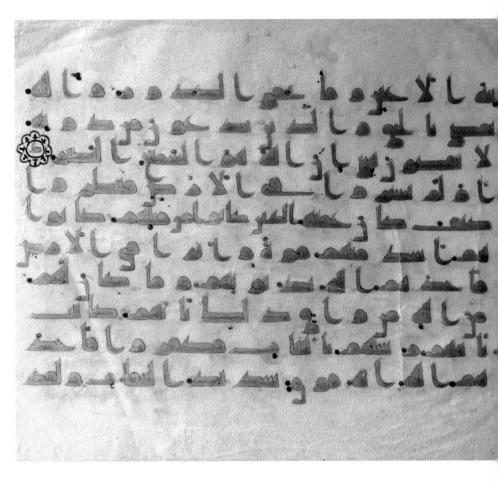

Arabic text from the Qur'an.

USING THE QUR'AN

Muslims recite parts of the Qur'an at prayer times, and learn this in Arabic, though it is translated into many languages. The sound of the original Arabic is said to be rhythmic and beautiful. Muhammad's companion, Umar, for example, was converted by hearing a few verses, saying that they had stormed his heart. Muslims aspire to learn the whole Qur'an by heart. Reading it can bring guidance and a sense of peace.

HADITH AND *SHARIAH*

Besides the Qur'an there are the many traditions about the deeds and words of Muhammad or other prophets such as Jesus. These traditions are the *hadith*. They are not revelation, but they are respected. The whole body of traditions about the life and wisdom of Muhammad is known as the *Sunnah*.

The *Shariah* is a body of laws or guidance that covers the six areas of religion, preserving life, inheritance, property, honour and intellect. The word means 'a path that leads to a well'. This body of law is gleaned from the Qur'an and the traditions of the community.

Following spread:
The Ka'aba at Makkah.

The one God

The first and most sacred Muslim belief is that there is only one God. The doctrine of unity, *tawhid*, refuses to associate any other being with God.

God is the Creator of all things, and one verse of the Qur'an might suggest something like the modern-day Big Bang theory, whereby the universe was once an infinitely small point of matter that exploded outwards:

'Have the unbelievers not beheld that the heavens and the earth were a solid mass, then We separated them; out of water we produced every living thing. Will they not believe, then?'

Sura 21:30

It is interesting, too, that living things are made up of about 50 to 90 per cent water, and that water is needed for all life.

Treasury of the Heart

'Prostrate yourselves before the Compassionate'.

Sura 25:60

Muslims teach that their faith is based on five pillars: the confession of faith (*Shahadah*), prayer (*salat*), almsgiving (*zakah*), fasting (*saum*), and pilgrimage (*hajj*).

THE *SHAHADAH*

The Muslim confession of faith is the *Shahadah*. This is: 'There is no god but God and Muhammad is His Messenger.' This is said by a convert to Islam in front of Muslim witnesses. In Arabic, it is *La ila' ha illallah Muhammad rasulullah.*

PRAYER

Muslims are commanded to pray five times a day using the set prayers, *salat*, and to say their own prayers, *du'a*. They will pray in the mosque, at home or wherever they are. They will stop in the street in Muslim countries and spread out their prayer mat, facing towards Makkah. The mat is kept clean and is a mark of respect to God. Mosques have a niche showing the direction of Makkah; this is called a *qibla*.

ALMSGIVING

Muslims are expected to pay a percentage of their annual income to charity. This *zakah* is usually 2.5 per cent, though farmers are expected to give 5 per cent of their produce. This goes towards the support of the mosques and Islamic education, as well as towards medical care and people in need. Muslims are exhorted to give to charity over and above this. As one *hadith* puts it, 'He is not a believer who eats his fill while his neighbour remains hungry by his side.' Muslims belong to a worldwide community, the *Ummah*.

FASTING

Fasting, *saum*, takes place during Ramadan, the ninth month of the Muslim calendar. This was the month in which Muhammad first received his revelations. The fast lasts for 29–30 days and takes place during daylight hours. Muslims can eat before dawn or after sunset. This is a spiritual discipline and expresses solidarity with the *Ummah*.

PILGRIMAGE

Hajj is a pilgrimage to Makkah which Muslims try to make at least once in their lifetimes. The *hajj* lasts five days and pilgrims – rich or poor – all dress in white robes.

BOOKS

God is believed to send down his message in Books. Jews and Christians are known as the people of the Book and are treated with respect. However, the Qur'an teaches that these earlier books have been changed and corrupted. Muslims believe that only the Qur'an is the pure Word of God.

PROPHETS

The Qur'an mentions twenty-five prophets by name, many of whom appear in the Bible. Muhammad is seen as the final prophet, the Seal of the Prophets.

ANGELS

Angels are mentioned frequently in the Qur'an. They bring God's message and record our deeds. They are the agents of God who protect people from evil and disaster. One passage says that they also pray for the forgiveness of all people:

'The heavens are rent asunder above them; while the angels proclaim the praise of their Lord and ask forgiveness for those on earth. Lo, God is truly the All-Forgiving, the Merciful.'

'By fasting during Ramadan,
and by giving *zakah*,
I feel part of a people,
a brotherhood, and it is
a great privilege.'
Faruq, a British Muslim

✳

Muslims prostrating themselves in formal prayer.

'God is the Greatest.
I bear witness that there
is no god but God.
I bear witness that
Muhammad is the
Messenger of God.
Come to prayer.
Come to what is good for you.
Prayer is better than sleep.
God is the Greatest.
There is no god but God.'

The Call to Prayer

'... celebrate the praise of
your Lord before the rising
of the sun and before its
setting; and glorify Him
during the hours of the night
and at the two ends of the
day, that you may be
well-pleased.'

Sura 20:130

✳

Prostration during prayer

Muslim prostrations during prayer are similar to
those of some Eastern Christians whom
Muhammad would have seen. He probably refers
to monks praying in *Sura* 24, when he describes
the prayers offered to God in holy houses, where
he is glorified three times a day:

> 'In houses God allowed to be raised to His
> Name to be mentioned therein, He is
> glorified therein, mornings and evenings.'
> **Sura** 24:36

The Christians of the Syrian area still pray in
this manner, and contemporary descriptions of
them sound like Muslim *salat*:

> 'The entire congregation began a long
> series of prostrations; from their standing
> position, the worshippers fell to their
> knees, and lowered their heads to the
> ground so that all that could be seen from
> the rear of the church was a line of
> upturned bottoms. All that distinguished
> the worship from that which might have
> taken place in a mosque was that the
> worshippers crossed and recrossed
> themselves as they performed their
> prostrations.'

William Dalrymple,
From the Holy Mountain

THE DAY OF JUDGEMENT

At the end of time will come the Day of
Judgement, when the intentions of all
hearts will be revealed. God will raise the
dead, a belief that was shockingly new
for Arabs in the seventh century CE. Only
God can judge as he knows the secrets of
our hearts; forgiveness has to be earned
through prayer and good actions.

Paths to Peace

*'Perform the prayer; give the
alms-tax and bow down with those
who bow down.'*

Sura 2:43

SALAT AND WUDU

Muslims are instructed to pray five times
a day. They pray at sunrise, noon, in the
afternoon, at sunset and at night. There
are set, prescribed prayers and
movements, which together are called
salat. Before saying these prayers, a
Muslim must wash, performing the *wudu*
ablutions:

✳ Both hands are washed up to the wrist.
✳ The mouth is rinsed out three times.
✳ The nostrils and tip of the nose are
washed three times.
✳ The face is washed three times,
moving from right to left and then
from the forehead down to the throat.
✳ The arms are washed three times.
✳ Water is passed over the head down to
the back of the neck.
✳ The ears are cleaned.
✳ The nape of the neck is cleaned.
✳ The feet are washed up to the ankles.

These elaborate rituals reflect the
conditions of the desert where Islam was
born and involve the parts of the body
that were dirtied by dust and sand.
Muslims believe it is respectful to come
before God externally clean in this way.

THE CALL TO PRAYER

In Muslim countries, a call to prayer will
be chanted from the mosques. This is led
by a *muezzin*. The early Muslim
community discussed the best way to call
to prayer, and they opted for the human
voice. The *muezzin* declares that there is

no God but God and that Muhammad is his prophet. The faithful are urged to come to prayer, for prayer is better than sleep. Some Westerners attest that the hauntingly beautiful prayer calls that echo and resonate around Muslim cities move them to tears.

FORMAL PRAYERS

Formal prayers are always in Arabic. Muslims stand to recite the opening *Sura* of the Qur'an, and then they bow three times, glorifying God. Then there are three prostrations with the forehead touching the ground. Prayers follow, with many recitations of *Allahu Akbar*, 'God is great.' Finally, kneeling with hands cupped open in supplication, Muslims can say their personal prayers, known as *du'a*. They can be in any language.

After all the movement in the mosque, there is a quiet, reverential hush as people whisper their own prayers.

THE NIGHT JOURNEY

During the night of the 27th day of Rajah, the seventh lunar month, Muhammad believed that he was shaken awake by Gabriel and told to sit upon a heavenly winged beast, the milk-white *Buraq*. He flew to Jerusalem, and from the site of the Temple mount, he ascended into heaven, the *Buraq* becoming a chariot of fire. He passed through the seven heavens and talked with God. Muhammad always believed that he had physically travelled that night, though some debate whether it was simply a vision granted to him.

Muhammad bargained with God to reduce the number of daily prayer times that were to be imposed upon believers to five.

MEDITATION

Muslims have prayer beads, *subha*, comprising 99 beads threaded on a string. These are to help Muslims recite the 99 names of God and serve as an aid to meditation and worship. Some Muslims say special prayers over and over again on the beads: 'Glory be to God', 'All praise be to God', and 'God is the greatest', 33 times each.

CHILDREN AND 'PRAYER BEARS'

Muslim children are taught the prayers from a young age. In recent years, imaginative games, books and toys have been produced for young children, such as Adam the Prayer Bear. As the advertisements say, 'He teaches as he's cuddled. Press him and he recites in English and Arabic.' Prayers include the *Bismillah* and *Allahu Akbar* among others.

Worship and the mosque

Mosques are literally 'places of prostration' and they are simple, plain buildings. They normally have a domed roof that helps sound to carry and a niche, *qibla*, set in the wall that points the way to Makkah. There are no statues or paintings of people or animals, lest these should encourage idolatry. Instead there are abstract patterns formed from Arabic verses from the Qur'an. The prayers are lead by an *imam*, 'one who stands in front'. *Imams* are specially trained and also preach to the worshippers at Friday prayers.

Men are encouraged to pray at the mosque when they can; women usually pray at home, but they can sit in a separate section or gallery at the mosque.

Awe and Wonder

> 'Prostrate yourselves before God, then, and worship Him.'
>
> *Sura* 53:62

THE MAJESTY OF GOD

The Qur'an repeatedly speaks of the majesty of God as Creator:

> '[He is] the Cleaver of the dawn; and He made the night a time of rest, and the sun and the moon a means of reckoning. Such is the ordering of God, the Mighty, the All-Knowing.'

> 'And it is He Who created the stars for you so as to be guided by them in the dark depths of the land and the sea. We have made plain the signs for a people who know.'
>
> *Sura* 6:96–97

Many Westerners honour and respect the faithfulness of Muslims who stop their jobs or their cars and prostrate themselves humbly, right where they are. They are completely unselfconscious about this.

Hagia Sophia in Istanbul. This was converted first from a church to a mosque and then from a mosque to a museum.

LORD OF THE WORLDS

The Qur'an teaches that God is the Lord of the Worlds, in different levels of reality. There are the seven heavens, and different orders of beings including the angels and the *jinn*. The *jinn* are created from fire and can act as messengers of God or work for evil. The devil, Iblis, is a *jinn* in the Qur'an (he is a fallen angel in the Bible, by contrast). He sinned when he refused to bow before Adam, the first man. 'It is not for me to prostrate myself to man, whom You created from sounding clay, from mud moulded into shape' (*Sura* 15:33).

SIGNS AND TREASURES

Muslims believe that God has a mysterious, hidden side ('God in Himself' or his 'Essence') and a revealed side. This is akin to rays of light emerging from the sun, and the rays of God are his 'attributes', his creative power manifested in a tree, a flower, a person. Creation is a book of signs given by God. Muslim tradition speaks of God revealing his attributes by creating the world; if he had not, they would remain hidden. They are spoken of as 'hidden treasure' or as 'storehouses', following the verse in the Qur'an:

> 'There is nothing for which We do not have the store-houses and sources, and We send it down only in a well-known measure.'
>
> *Sura* 15:21

The chief part of the treasure, of the storehouses, are the 99 Beautiful Names, with all the creative power they embody.

The self

There is a wonder about the nature of the self. Muslims see this as having three parts, the *Nafs*, the *Ruh* and the *Qalb*. The *Nafs* is the emotional part of us, the *Ruh* is the spiritual, and the *Qalb* is the heart, the organ of perception within ourselves. Often, an analogy of a horse and rider is used. The *Nafs* is a wild horse that is tamed by the rider (*Ruh*) who, in turn, receives strength from the *Qalb*.

The Qur'an does not seek to deny or eradicate the *Nafs* entirely, but to tame it. Emotions and passions are a vital part of being human, but they must not control people:

> 'Do you see him who has taken his fancy as his god?'
>
> *Sura* 25:43

Another resounding example of the mystery and power of God in the Qur'an is the resurrection of the dead. This is seen as an extension of God's power to let things 'Be':

> 'God… brings the dead to life and He has power over everything. And that Hour is coming, no doubt about it; and that God raises up those who are in their graves.'
>
> *Sura* 22:6–7

This was the belief of Jews and Christians before Muhammad, but the pagan Arabs had little time for hopes about the afterlife. It was new to them.

'I looked at the stars in the night sky and saw how vast they were. A Muslim worker with me bowed down and said his prayers by the camp fire. I was filled with admiration and wonder…'
Comment made by a Swedish convert to Islam

'Indeed, when We want a thing to be, We just say to it, "Be," and it comes to be.'
Sura 16:40

✳

*Egyptian Sufis celebrate on the
evening of the Prophet's birthday.*

Journey into Mystery

*'He is with you, wherever you are:
God perceives whatever you do.'*

Sura 57:4

REFUSAL OF SYMBOLS

Islam has no sacred symbols or
sacraments. There is no ordained
priesthood, only the trained *imams*,
who are lay-leaders in Christian terms.

Abstract patterns and banners are formed from Arabic writing, taking the names of God or verses from the Qur'an. There are no symbols because Muslims refuse pictorial decoration of their places of worship.

The *Ka'aba* in Makkah is a sacred place, a holy object. This is thought to have been the first house of prayer ever built by Adam, and then rebuilt years later by Abraham. It is reverently circled, and the black stone set in its walls is kissed by Muslim pilgrims.

The idea of a 'house' is extended to cover the whole of Islam. The whole Muslim community, the *Ummah*, is known as *Dar al-Islam*, the 'House of Islam'.

RITES OF PASSAGE

The set *salat* prayers contain beautiful symbols of adoration and humility, with the bowing and prostrations, but apart from these, there is very little that is ritualistic in Islam. Birth ceremonies involve whispering *Allahu akbar* in a newborn baby's ear. There is also a naming ceremony, *aqueeqah*, where a boy's name is taken from one of the names of God or the prophets and a girl's name is taken from a well-known Muslim woman. Boys will be circumcised at *aqueeqah*. Circumcision is practised by Jews too, following on from the practice of Abraham.

THE SUFIS

The Sufis are a group who follow the mystical strand that is present in the Qur'an. They believe that God is Reality, and that all created things are from him and will return to him: 'Unto God all affairs are returned' (*Sura* 2:210). The doctrine of return, *ma'ad*, opens up a quest for union and harmony with the divine. Sufis speak of life as a dance between God and the soul. They sometimes practise a dance that seeks to attune them to the spiritual. Mainstream, orthodox Muslims tend to treat this with suspicion.

The Sufis have also exalted Jesus as 'the Seal of Love' whereas Muhammad is the Seal of the Prophets.

Mystics seek to get back to the knowledge of God that the soul had before it left his 'storehouse' and was revealed upon earth.

Making Merry

> *'It is a duty to God incumbent on those who can, to make the pilgrimage to the House...'*
>
> *Sura* 3:97

RAMADAN

Ramadan is the month of fasting from sunrise to sunset. Cafes in Muslim countries will have full tables, with people reading newspapers and chatting, but only foreign, non-Muslim visitors will order food. Muslims are exempt from the fast if:

* they are under twelve years old
* they are elderly
* they are pregnant or breastfeeding a baby
* they have to travel over 50 miles
* they are ill.

Ramadan was the month during which the Qur'an was revealed. One night is specially commemorated during the fast, *Laylat ul Qadr* (Night of Power), when the Qur'an was first revealed to

Indian Muslim girls hug after morning prayer in Calcutta. They are celebrating the festival of Id-ul-Fitr which marks the end of the holy month of Ramadan.

Muhammad on Mount Hira. This is celebrated on one of the odd-numbered days in the last ten days of Ramadan.

ID-UL-FITR

Id is Arabic for festival. Islam has two major festivals, *Id-ul-Fitr* and *Id-ul-Adha*. They are times of rejoicing and feasting. *Id-ul-Fitr* comes at the end of the month of Ramadan, on the first day of the next month. It was instituted by Muhammad himself, and it is a time of celebration after the fasting finishes. In a Muslim country it will be a national holiday and people will visit family and friends, often wearing their best or new clothes. Gifts are given to the poor, and presents are shared with friends. *Id-ul-Fitr* begins in the mosque with shared prayer.

ID-UL-ADHA

Id-ul-Adha means 'festival of sacrifice', and it was also instituted by Muhammad. It recalls the story of Abraham sacrificing his son (Ishmael in the Qur'an; Isaac in the Bible). This *Id* comes towards the end of the pilgrimage to Makkah, the *hajj*. It is a public holiday in Muslim countries.

The festival begins in the mosque. A sheep or a goat is often sacrificed by each family in memory of the story of Abraham, though a cow or a camel can be offered as well. God does not want the animal, as such, but he does demand devotion and service. The animal is shared out between the family, any guests and the poor. Special prayers for forgiveness may also be said.

Today

> *'This Qur'an could never have been produced except by God…There is no doubt about it. It is from the Lord of the Worlds.'*
>
> *Sura* 10:37

JIHAD

Islam faces a crisis of identity in the Western world because of extremist groups and regular media images of terrorist action. The term *jihad* is often

> 'The Night of Power is better than a thousand months, The angels and the Spirit descend thereon by the Leave of their Lord with every Command. It is peace, till the break of dawn.'
>
> **Sura** 97:3–5

> 'It was an amazing, moving experience. You are part of a great crowd, moving along and praying. It makes your faith strong, to believe with so many others.'
>
> Musa, a young man from Morocco, talking about **Hajj**

 ### Hajj

The pagan Arabs came to Makkah each year on pilgrimage. They circled the *Ka'aba* and offered sacrifices on the black stone. This was probably a fertility ritual. Muhammad cleansed the *hajj* of pagan customs and associations and made it thoroughly monotheistic. *Hajj* takes place during the twelfth Islamic month, and about 2 million Muslims from all corners of the globe come to Makkah.

The first part of the pilgrimage is for male pilgrims to don white pilgrim robes as they approach Makkah. These are made of two sheets of unsewn white cloth. Women wear ordinary clothes, but their bodies must be completely covered.

The *hajj* lasts for five days. This begins with circling the *Ka'aba* seven times, starting at the black stone, which is reverently kissed or touched. Then the pilgrims go to two small hills nearby. They walk quickly between these two places, remembering the suffering of Abraham's servant

Hagar and her son, Ishmael. She was searching for water at this spot, according to Muslim belief.

Then a day is spent in the valley of Arafat among special tents, meditating upon Allah all day. Part of the evening is spent collecting forty-nine small stones. Pilgrims spend the night in Muzdalifah.

In Mina, the pilgrims gather at the site of three ancient stone pillars. Muslims believe that this is where Ishmael drove the devil away by throwing stones, and the pilgrims throw their stones at the pillars as a symbol of turning from evil.

After this, animals are sacrificed for *Id-ul-Adha*. A man can then be called a *hajji* and a woman a *hajja*.

On the *hajj*, Muslims will meet members of the same faith from all over the world. The American Black Rights leader, Malcolm X, left the Nation of Islam movement in the 1960s after going on *hajj* and realizing that white people could be fellow believers and brothers.

erroneously translated as 'holy war'. It actually means 'struggle', and most usages in the Qur'an are about either a personal struggle against sin, or injustice in society. The faithful Muslim should struggle against exploitation and tyranny, and immorality such as pornography. The duty to strive for what is good echoes throughout the Qur'an, and it is clearly stated in *Sura* 90. There, two highways are revealed, one easy and one rocky. The latter involves:

> '*The freeing of a slave;*
> *Or feeding, upon a day of famine,*
> *An orphan near of kin,*
> *Or a destitute man in dire need.*
> *Then, being one of those who believe,*
> *command steadfastness to each other*
> *and command compassion.*'
>
> *Sura* 90:13–17

Jihad can involve armed struggle, but the Qur'an always uses the term in conjunction with *qital*, meaning 'fighting'. There are strict conditions to allow this:
* fighting in self-defence
* fighting to free the oppressed
* fighting for the freedom of faith where Islam is persecuted.

It would be more accurate to speak of 'just war' here, rather than 'holy war', as in the Christian tradition. While many Muslims are peace-loving, there are extremists who take the teaching on *jihad* out of context and apply the idea of fighting for the faith against other religions and nations. Ironically, though, Muhammad became more of a warrior and commander in his later years than a religious leader until Arabia was at peace and Islam held sway.

THE MARTYR TRADITION

The idea of martyrdom in Islam, *shaheed*, means 'to have witnessed' to the faith. It does not necessarily apply to someone who dies on the battlefield. A mother who died in childbirth would be *shaheed* because she had been struggling to bring new life into the world. *Shaheed* must not be sought after for its own sake, or for personal glory or revenge. Qur'anic prohibitions on harming women, children and aged men in warfare are seen to outlaw acts of terrorism such as 9/11 or suicide bombers, no matter if their cause might be justified in the eyes of some.

JEWS AND CHRISTIANS

The Qur'an respects Jews and Christians as 'people of the Book' and emphasizes that Christians are particularly close in friendship. Jews are an exalted nation, Jesus and Mary are honoured, and the *Torah* and the Gospels were sent down from heaven. There are some passages that suggest a less conciliatory stance, though. One such is the demand that the men of the people of the Book living under Muslim control pay a tax, the *jizya*. This is properly understood as a tax to exempt them from fighting in a war, as it would not be fair to ask them to defend Islam.

There are passages that warn about unbelievers among the people of the Book. This is about particular individuals who were aggressive and fought against Muhammad. For example, *Sura* 60:8–9 asks for compassion on non-Muslims who do not fight against the faith, but resistance to those who do. More moderate Muslims appeal to these verses to form a culture of respect and

Shariah and ijtihad

The body of traditional Muslim law is derived from many sources, such as the Qur'an, *hadith*, the consensus of scholars in the community and jurisprudence.

Many traditions were set down in ancient times, in medieval culture, and there are debates about applying some of these laws today. Muslim scholars can work with varying traditions and new situations to derive what they feel is the will of God today. They compare cases and tease out ideas, using independent reasoning. This is *ijtihad,* and this independent reasoning allowed the Muslim world to blossom in a golden age of civilization between about 750 and 1250 CE, with the birth of the university and algebra, musical inventions such as the guitar, translations of Greek philosophers that were lost in the West and advances in medical science. This free and widespread use of *ijtihad* was stopped by the Caliph of Baghdad in the Middle Ages when political tensions, Muslim in-fighting and a rival Caliph from Spain threatened the unity of Islam. Muslim civilization went into decline. Many Muslims today are seeking to practise *ijtihad* for the twenty-first century.

toleration. Some see a distinction between the Makkan period and the Madinan period of revelation, with sterner words for Jews and Christians in the latter. The above explanation should be sufficient, but some more extreme Muslims take the later, sterner injunctions as a licence to dishonour Jews and Christians.

THE ROLE OF WOMEN

In many ways, if the text of the Qur'an is studied clearly, women have equal rights to men. The Adam and Eve story asserts this forcefully in that the couple are created separately (that is, the woman is not made from the man) and both are equally responsible for falling into temptation. Eve is blessed with childbearing, not cursed.

Women have equal rights under the law, a right to hold property and to work. They also have a right to inheritance, but this is usually half that of men. This is because women are not expected to provide for the family financially. It is true that a wife is expected to put the care of her family first, before any work, but she is entitled to assistance and an education if she so desires. The above is the true and primitive teaching in the Qur'an but there are different attitudes and cultural customs in the Muslim world. Thus women cannot drive a car or walk outside without a male companion in Saudi Arabia, but they can do both in nearby Kuwait.

However, divorce is assumed to be the prerogative of the man. The Qur'an allows a Muslim man to have as many as four wives so long as he can afford to keep them, and he must treat them fairly. This was written for a very different culture from many nations today, and many Muslims have just one wife. Polygamy is a heated issue for some, though, and it is sometimes pointed out that Muhammad had more than the Quranic limit of wives – he had several wives and concubines. His youngest (and dearest), Aisha, he married when she was only nine. His behaviour is seen as an exception, as the Prophet's reward.

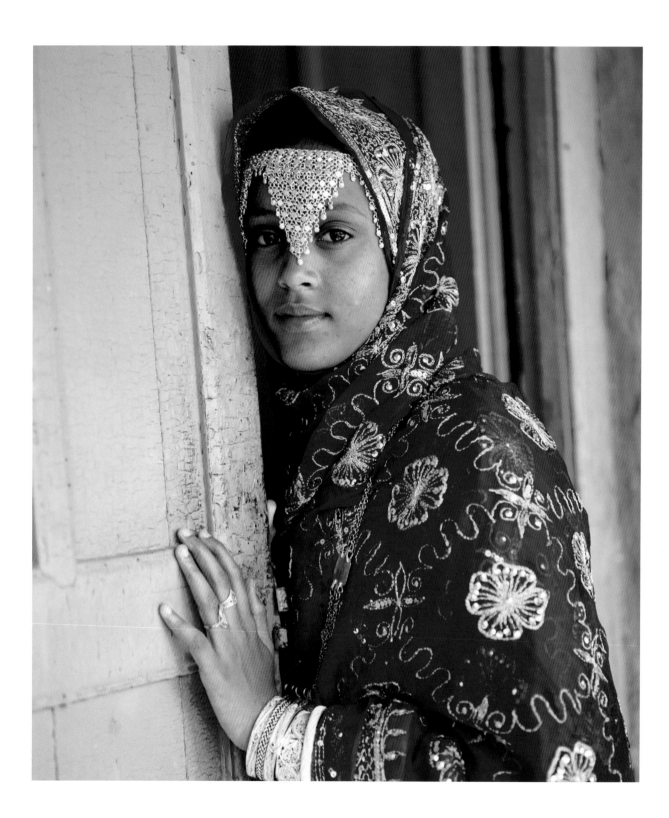

Dress codes and modesty laws are a source of debate. The Qur'an does tell women to lower their eyes when out in public, but men are also told to lower theirs when meeting women. The tradition of covering the head and the entire body apart from the hands and feet is an interpretation of *Sura* 24:31: 'And let them drape their bosoms with their veils and not show their finery except to their husbands…' and also other close male relatives.

This verse is open to other interpretations and might mean covering their chest only. Different Muslims and cultures have interpreted this *Sura* differently. Many Western Muslim women seek to understand it as liberally as possible. Having said that, some Muslim women delight in being fully veiled as this feels safe and protects their modesty.

There are tensions and debates, and Islamic feminists such as journalist Irshad Manji in Canada defend the right of Muslim women to think freely.

'Men and women who have submitted, believed, obeyed, are truthful, steadfast, guarding their private parts and remembering Allah often…'
Sura 33:35

'Let none of you fall upon his wife like a donkey falls upon a she donkey.'
Hadith of Muhammad

'What if a Western coalition of Muslims and non-Muslims endowed women in the Islamic world to own and manage local TV stations? What if Oprah Winfrey led the coalition?… What the printing press did for the Protestant reformation – relax the stranglehold on knowledge – indie TV channels can do for Islam.'
Irshad Manji,
The Trouble with Islam

✳

ISLAM	at a glance...

- ♦ When did it begin? – Muslims believe that Islam has always been taught by God's true prophets throughout history. Islam as we know it appeared in the seventh century CE in Arabia.
- ♦ The founder – Muslims believe that the first prophet of God was Adam, the first man. Muhammad taught Islam in Arabia in the seventh century CE (c. 570–632).
- ♦ God – There is one God only who is known as Allah in Arabic. (This simply means 'the One God'.)
- ♦ Redeemer figure – There is no redeemer in Islam. Muhammad is just a prophet. Muslims believe that you have to earn your own salvation and forgiveness from God by following his guidance and commandments.
- ♦ Scriptures – The Qur'an, as revealed to Muhammad in a series of revelations and oracles. Muslims believe that there were earlier books such as the Psalms and the Gospels, but that these must have become corrupted over the years as their teachings clash in some ways with those of the Qur'an.

- ♦ Beliefs – There is one God, and he sends his angels to help humanity and his prophets to guide them. Muhammad is the final prophet. There is a Day of Judgement and a resurrection from the dead.
- ♦ Place of worship – The mosque is a 'place of prostration', which is simply decorated. There is a niche pointing to Makkah, and Muslims assemble in rows to bow down in worship.
- ♦ Sacred food – There is no sacramental or special food used in Islam. There is a month of fasting during sunlight hours, during Ramadan. There is also a meal of mutton or goat, shared with family and friends, at *Id ul-Adha*. Certain foods are forbidden, *haram*, such as pork.
- ♦ Main festivals – *Id ul-Fitr* comes at the end of Ramadan; *Id ul-Adha* comes at the end of the pilgrimage to Makkah.
- ♦ Key symbols – the crescent moon and rising star; the Ka'aba in Makkah as the holiest place; Arabic names for God or the prophets.

Left hand page: A young Muslim woman wearing the hijab.

Zoroastrianism and Baha'i

*'O Wise Lord, Zarathustra here choses for himself
thy Spirit which is the most holy...'*

The prophet Zarathustra

Iran is now mainly a Muslim country. Of
course, there are various other faiths
represented among its population,
including an ancient Christian church.
There is also a faith that is much more
ancient than either Christianity or Islam,
and one that is relatively new. The
ancient faith is Zoroastrianism; the
recent one that of the Baha'i movement.

ZOROASTRIANISM

The ancient faith of Persia is named
after a prophet about whom very little
is known. The Greek version of his
name is Zoroaster, but the more
correct spelling would be Zarathustra.
Scholars debate when he lived, though
the Zoroastrians themselves date his
life quite specifically and start their
calendar from the date of his vision
of God on 5 May 630 BCE (this being
1 AR, the first 'Year of Religion').
Most scholars, however, would place
his birth much earlier, in around the
year 1200 BCE. Many Westerners
have heard his name because of the
work of the nineteenth-century
philosopher, Nietzsche. He used
the figure of the prophet to mouth
his own aphorisms in *Also Sprach
Zarathustra*. The prophet in this

work says things far removed from the historical Zarathustra's sentiments, though. Nietzsche was declaring the death of God.

By the time of King Cyrus the Great in the sixth century BCE, Zoroastrianism was the main religion practised in Persia. Persian society was devastated by the conquest of Alexander the Great (or 'the Accursed' in Persian legend) in the fourth century BCE. It was revived under the Parthian dynasty, which was able to stand up to the might of Rome. The Sasanian dynasty developed the faith much further, collecting writings and advancing theological orthodoxy from the fourth to the seventh centuries CE. Then the nation fell to Islam. Gradually, Zoroastrianism declined and was suppressed, meaning there are only a small number of adherents left in Iran today. Sometime during the eighth to tenth centuries CE, a group migrated from Persia to escape Muslim rule. At first they went to Hormuz in the Gulf region and then to India where they were known as 'Parsees' (or 'Persians').

Altogether there are between 150,000 and 200,000 adherents of Zoroastrianism in the world today. This is a small number for an ancient faith that once held great sway and influence. Aspects of the ancient faith might have coloured the Iranian version of Islam, however.

The genius

Zoroastrianism was an early form of monotheism that shook up existing religious ideas. Gods were demoted to the ranks of angels and demons, and the hope of a resurrection of the dead stood out from traditional views of the time.

The symbol

Ahura Mazda, the Wise Lord, rides the solar disk with outstretched wings. He is the light of the dawn. It is said that after a period of meditation, Zarathustra watched the sun set and saw the power of light and dark in the world.

BAHA'I

The Baha'i movement began in the nineteenth century as a sect of Islam, rather as Christianity began as a Jewish sect. In 1844, a Shi'ite Muslim called himself the Bab, meaning 'gate', and declared that he was a manifestation of God and the Twelfth *Imam*, the *Madhi*. He was executed publicly in 1850. One of his followers renamed himself Baha'u'llah ('the Glory of God') and claimed to be the coming teacher foretold by the Bab. He also claimed to be a manifestation of God. In 1892, his son Abd al-Baha ('Servant of the Glory') took over. He did not, interestingly, claim to be a divine manifestation. He travelled widely, promulgating Baha'u'llah's teachings, going to the USA in 1912. His grandson, Shogi Effendi (1897–1957), carried on the leadership until his death, and then it passed into the hands of a council of elected representatives, the Universal House of Justice, though there is a breakaway group, the Orthodox Baha'i faith.

Baha'is have a sense of the unity of all faiths, with essential truths present in each one. They believe in nine manifestations of God through human teachers. They also have lofty ideals for world peace and development.

By the year 2000 it was reckoned that there were over 6 million Baha'is worldwide, spread throughout many

The symbol of Ahura Mazda at ancient Persepolis.

countries. The international headquarters are in Haifa, Jerusalem.

The genius

The Baha'i faith is an attempt to unify all faiths, trying to take each one seriously by seeing it as a fitting revelation for its own time.

The symbol

The temples on each continent have nine sides. These represent the nine manifestations of God. Nine-pointed stars are also found on jewellery, books and gravestones.

Zoroastrianism

'To what land shall I flee, wither to flee? From the nobles and from my peers I am cut off, nor do the people love me, nor the liar rulers of the land.'

Yasna 46:1

FIRST STEPS

There is little known about the historical Zarathustra (Zoroaster in Greek). Scholars debate when he lived and place him anywhere from 1500 to 1000 BCE in the Late Bronze Age. Zoroastrian tradition itself dates him '258 years before Alexander', which would give him

A Zoroastrian fire ceremony.

demons before they went into exile, but these ideas emerged in a renewed and developed way later on. It is significant that the only pagan ruler to be honoured as blessed by Yahweh in the Hebrew Bible was Cyrus of Persia ('Thus says the Lord to his anointed, to Cyrus, whose right hand I have held' [Isaiah 45:1]), and it was *magi* from the East who came to worship at the crib of the infant Jesus. Speculation abounds as to who these men were – Babylonian astrologers, Jews, or Zoroastrian magi, recognizing the birth of the expected Saviour?

Baha'i

> *'The earth is but one country and mankind its citizens.'*
>
> *Gleanings from the Writings of Baha'u'llah*

FIRST STEPS

Mirza Ali Muhammad (1819–50) became the Bab in 1844. At first, the Bab claimed to teach a new form of Islam and to be the returned Twelfth *Imam*, the *Madhi*. In 1848, the Babis, his followers, declared their independence from Islam and struggled with the Persian authorities. The Bab was executed in 1850 after being accused of treason for plotting against the *Shah*.

The Bab had predicted a new teacher who would carry on and expand his teaching. Mirza Husayn Ali Nuri (1817–92) was one of the Bab's loyal followers. He was imprisoned in 1852 in a notorious dungeon, the Siyah-Chal ('Black Pit'), beneath a square in central Tehran. It had been the sump of a public bath. He was there for four months in an unbearable stench. It was here that he claimed a personal revelation that convinced him that he was the new manifestation of God to come. He became Baha'u'llah.

THE GOAL

Baha'u'llah taught that there was only one God behind all faiths. The manifestations of God on earth were like the rays of the sun. All Baha'is agree that there have been nine manifestations, but there is a slight dispute over who they were. The main list has Adam, Abraham, the Buddha, Krishna, Moses, Jesus, Muhammad, the Bab and Baha'u'llah. Variations would take out the Buddha and Krishna, putting in Noah and Zarathustra, or two Arabian prophets.

There are different degrees or dispensations of revelation according to Baha'u'llah. Each stage is incomplete but appropriate for the age when it was given. Thus, there is truth in all Scriptures, but there are differences and disagreements. Earlier teachings have to be interpreted in the light of later ones, especially those of the Bab and Baha'u'llah.

Besides the idea of the oneness of God, there is a strong belief in the brotherhood of humanity.

TEACHERS OF THE WAY

Baha'u'llah wrote over 100 books, and there are many other commentaries by later followers. The most important Scripture is *Kitab-i-Aqdas*, the 'Most Holy Book'.

TREASURY OF THE HEART

The created universe is seen as an emanation of God and not as created out

> 'The Ancient Beauty hath consented to be bound with chains that mankind may be released from its bondage… he hath drained to its dregs the cup of sorrow, that all the peoples of the earth may attain unto abiding joy, and be filled with gladness.'
>
> **Gleanings from the Writings of Baha'u'llah**

> 'So powerful is the light of unity that it can illuminate the whole earth.'
>
> Baha'u'llah, **Epistle to the Son of the Wolf**

> 'They have been sent down, and their Books were revealed, for the purpose of promoting the knowledge of God, and of furthering unity and fellowship among men.'
>
> Baha'u'llah, **Epistle to the Son of the Wolf**

❊

of nothing, *ex nihilo*, as in Judaism, Christianity and Islam. The universe is eternal, a never-ending emanation from God. There is a strong pantheistic vision in the Baha'i faith.

There is a belief in an afterlife as a disembodied existence, though traditional descriptions of heaven and hell are seen as highly symbolic. Judgement is self-brought; the soul that looks after itself enters bliss, while the soul that has neglected the light of God will have pain.

PATH TO PEACE

Baha'u'llah taught that people had twin duties; they must recognize God's messenger of the day and obey every ordinance set out by him. Baha'is have very high ideals about universal development and education, urging the use of a common language such as Esperanto, equal opportunities for both genders, universal peace and a world government to foster these hopes.

AWE AND WONDER

Baha'is have to say three special prayers a day once they reach the age of spiritual responsibility at 15. One of them might be the following:

'I bear witness, O my God, that Thou has created me to know Thee and to worship Thee. I testify at this moment to my powerlessness and to Thy might, to my poverty and to Thy wealth. There is none other God but Thee, the Help in Peril, the Self-Subsisting.'

A Baha'i temple in New Delhi.

- ◆ When did it begin? – in the nineteenth century CE in Persia, now Iran.
- ◆ The founder – the Bab ('gate') in 1844 and his successor, Baha'u'llah, in 1852.
- ◆ God – There is one God behind all faiths.
- ◆ Redeemer figure – There are no redeemers, only teachers, such as the Bab and Bah'u'llah.
- ◆ Scriptures – All Scriptures of all faiths are revered, though the writings of Baha'u'llah are central, especially the *Kitab-i-Aqdas*.
- ◆ Beliefs – The universe is an emanation of God, eternally in existence. God has sent nine messengers over the ages, ending with Baha'u'llah.
- ◆ Place of worship – Baha'is meet in local halls, but each continent has a nine-sided temple, remembering the nine messengers.
- ◆ Sacred food – There are no special foods, but feasts are important, such as the Nineteen Day Feast.
- ◆ Festivals – *Ridvan* is a twelve-day feast remembering the calling of Baha'u'llah. The Nineteen Day Feast assembles Baha'is to renew links and to consider community matters.
- ◆ Key symbols – the nine-sided temples.

Prayer is made facing Acre in the East, the site of Baha'u'llah's tomb.

Baha'i worship consists of prayers and readings with music, and a wide variety of styles is permitted. Local Spiritual Assemblies plan and approve the worship. Each continent has a nine-sided temple, representing the nine manifestations of God. These places are known as a 'Dawning Place of the Praise of God'.

JOURNEY INTO MYSTERY

Baha'is do not have a priesthood or any sacraments. There are no special initiation ceremonies. One important activity that encourages spiritual growth is the 'Baha'i consultation'. Assemblies, families and friends use these to meet together for prayer. Then they set out the facts of a matter as they understand them and discuss differences. They seek out a spark of truth, a convergence and a consensus.

MAKING MERRY

There are various festivals relating to the teachers, such as the Bab's foretelling of the coming of Baha'u'llah. This is the twelve-day festival of *Ridvan* ('paradise'). There is a regular Nineteen Day Feast for all ages, in which local assemblies meet to discuss news and consult with each other.

TODAY

Baha'is in Iran are a persecuted minority who are not given the status of 'people of the Book' (as Jews and Christians are). Since the founders separated from Islam, the movement is seen as heretical and treated with suspicion. In other parts of the world they are involved in educational and development programmes, and attend UN summits.

Confucianism, Taoism and Shinto

'Devotion to one's duties as a subject, and respect for the spirits while keeping them at a distance, may be called wisdom.'

Confucius, The Analects

Chinese society remained fairly static for many centuries, reflecting the social structure and the unchanging nature of the Chinese language. There was no state religion and although people believed in the gods, they were more remote and less important than the veneration of the family ancestors. Moral and social codes for this life were paramount. Chinese civilization goes back millennia. Three dominant systems of thought or faiths became central to Chinese life. One of these, Buddhism, was an import. The other two were Confucianism and Taoism. Chinese traditional religions are still said to have 225 million adherents.

Japan had an ancient folk religion with many deities reflecting the various islands of the nation. It was only named

Shinto in the sixth century CE to distinguish it from the recent imports of Confucianism and Buddhism.

CONFUCIANISM

Confucius, or K'ung-fu-Tzu (551–479 BCE), did not teach as a prophet or religious reformer. He was more of an ethicist and philosopher. He seemed agnostic about the gods, but he admitted that he felt his system had come from the authority of heaven (*Tian*). He taught a rigid, thorough social code of behaviour that sought to maintain harmony in society.

Confucius worked against a background of social upheaval. The first great dynasty of kings, the *Shang*, had given way to the *Chou*. State corruption was rife. Various schools of thought flourished to try to remedy the situation. This lasted until 200 BCE and was known as the time of the Hundred Schools.

The genius

An ethical and social system that side-stepped religious debates and looked at roles between people in society. Honour and respect for one another were vital.

TAOISM

Taoism goes back millennia into the origins of Chinese civilization. It merges ancient folk rituals and beliefs with a sensitive mysticism about life energy, the Way and working in harmony with nature. The most highly regarded teacher is one Lao Tzu, whom tradition locates in the sixth century BCE. Taoism emerged from the time of the Hundred Schools to seek an answer to social ills that was distinct from the teachings of Confucius. This was a way of starting with nature and observing her rhythms and flows, seeking to live within these and not to impose false order upon them. Taoism is more mystical and passive than prescriptive, rational Confucianism.

The genius

Taoism allowed a common spiritual focus, no matter what local deities or rituals one followed. The Tao was universal and indefinable.

SHINTO

Shinto is the prehistoric belief and ritual system of Japan, dating back centuries. It pre-dated the arrival of Buddhism and Christianity. It is often translated as 'the way of the gods', and it is an animistic and polytheistic system that is part of the lives of many Japanese. It coexists with Buddhism as people move from one ritual to another: Buddhism deals with the ancestors and funerals, whereas Shinto deals with everyday life including the celebration of birth and marriage. 95 per cent of the Japanese population claim to practise Shinto while 75 per cent claim to be Buddhist.

The genius

An ancient system of honouring heavenly powers and spending time to be rapt in awe at the wonder of nature.

BUDDHISM

China and Japan saw the formation of two distinctive forms of Buddhism, *Ch'an* or Zen, going back to the sixth century CE. Japan also saw the rise of *Nichiren* Buddhism, with its repeated chant of *namo myoho renge kyo*.

CHRISTIANITY

Christianity came to China and the Far East much earlier than has been believed. Later Western missionaries followed in the footsteps of earlier teachers and monks. In 1625, workmen digging a grave near Xian in China unearthed a large stone stela with an ancient inscription that told of the coming of the Christians as early as 635 CE. Later, at the end of the nineteenth century, a Taoist priest unearthed a cache of old scrolls in a bricked-up room that had been sealed since 1005 CE. Besides Buddhist and Taoist texts, there were Christian ones, speaking of Jesus in Eastern terms such as the 'Jade-Faced One' and the 'One Sacred Spirit'. This showed that Christian monks had followed the old silk routes from Persia and had established communities and monasteries in China that flourished for many years.

Confucianism

'Devotion to one's duties as a subject, and respect for the spirits while keeping them at a distance, may be called wisdom.'

Confucius, *Analects* vi.20

FIRST STEPS

Confucius has left little sure detail about his life except that he came from a noble family and that he worked in the civil service of a provincial king. He was removed from this position when he was 50, and then he wandered about gathering disciples as an itinerant teacher. His disciples were the reason that we have heard of him. They collected his sayings and circulated them, along with others, for years to come. The unchanging nature of the Chinese language for millennia meant that such a transmission was possible.

A cult of Confucius grew up after his death, whereby his memory was revered. Legends abounded, such as that he had written every ancient Chinese text. The

K'ung-fu-Tzu.

Han dynasty, in the second century BCE, made his teaching the official state ideology, presumably because they prospered under its stability.

His system became normative for Chinese, Japanese and Korean society.

THE GOAL

Confucius sought social harmony to heal the state. He preached the principle of *Yin/Yang*, contrasting opposites that formed a balance. This taught a passive acceptance of one's status and role in the family and society, giving in to tradition and also fulfilling certain duties. He taught the 'silver rule' of 'Do not do unto others what you do not want them to do unto you.' This was based upon respect and the desire for social harmony rather than an ethic of compassion.

TEACHERS OF THE WAY

Confucius did not believe that he taught any new doctrines. He considered himself 'a transmitter and not an originator, trusting in and loving the ancients' (*Analects* vii.1).

The *Analects* are a collection of the aphorisms of Confucius, and the teachings of his disciples and illustrative incidents from their lives. They are short, pithy sayings and not long dialogues.

TREASURY OF THE HEART

Confucius spoke of two virtues, *jen* and *li*. *Jen* is righteousness within, or harmony between people. *Li* is social etiquette, the rituals and mores required to express and help create harmony. Confucius believed that *jen* and *li* depended upon each other; *jen* without *li* would be vague and powerless, while *li* without *jen* would be empty and rigid.

Though Confucius tried to keep a strict social order in place, he also revealed a radical streak, which some of his disciples developed further. He took the concept of the nobleman, the *chun-tzu*, and argued that any person who practised *jen* and *li*, having these virtues in their lives, was the true *chun-tzu*. This challenged corrupt rulers and elders who should have shown their service, and the values of duty as befitting their status. This idea was developed further by Mencius (371–289 BCE). He argued that it was the moral duty of the people to overthrow a corrupt ruler, as a corrupt ruler was no more than a 'commoner'.

He explained this about the overthrow of the last *Shang* emperor, Chou:

'A robber and a ruffian should be called a commoner. I have heard that they punished the commoner Chou, but I have not heard that they murdered their ruler.'

Mencius xvi.8

PATHS TO PEACE

Social harmony depended upon filial respect and duty. The family was the basic unit, with father showing kindness to son, son showing filial respect to father. The older brother should show gentility to the younger, who needed to show humility in return. A husband had to be righteous in his actions towards his wife, who would then be obedient. Older people should be considerate to the younger ones, who would then defer to their elders.

A ruler should serve and care for his subjects, who would then give him loyalty in return. One of Confucius's sayings reflects his value of the sage emperor. He spoke of one who had so much wisdom and virtue that he did not need to take any action; his influence was secure:

> *'Was not Shun one who ruled without action? For what action did he take? He did nothing but sit reverently facing due south.'*
>
> *Analects* xv.4

A key idea was filial piety, *xian*, which was the social cohesion of any family. This would mean that parents should be honoured even if they were unreasonable, and the ancestors were included in this scheme, even though they were dead. Nothing should be done to bring dishonour to their memories.

There were mixed blessings in this as a certain routine and rigidity was maintained, but there was harmony, mutual responsibility and an encouragement of learning as the principles of Confucianism were passed on.

AWE AND WONDER

Ritual was important to Confucius, not in any mystical sense, but as a way of encoding values. Rituals to honour the ancestors were encouraged for this reason.

JOURNEY INTO MYSTERY

There was no metaphysical speculation in the work of Confucius, just a desire for harmony. Following his precepts and social etiquette resulted in social cohesion and mutual responsibility. In traditional Chinese society, no one is forced to follow the principles of Confucius; they are literally shamed into doing so when all around them disdain their actions and shun them.

Confucius believed that social harmony and personal virtue would have an almost magical influence on the world and nature around us. This, to an extent, is behind his saying about the Emperor Shun above, and also his answer to a question about the meaning of an ancient ritual:

> *'I do not know. Could not one who knows its meaning deal with the Empire as though he were turning it over here?'* [He pointed to the palm of his hand.]
>
> *Analects* iii.11

MAKING MERRY

Confucius is honoured as a revered ancestor and teacher. Rituals are held to celebrate his teachings, such as the *Chongmyo* rites.

TODAY

Confucianism in modern China has suffered from the rise of Communism. The rigid social hierarchies and duties were attacked by Mao as thwarting the power of the workers. Yet some aspects of the system were taken over into Maoism. Mao's thoughts were revered and written down in little red books, and leaders were expected to set examples to secure the loyalty and commitment of the people.

In the West, Chinese communities find that the traditional ways are being eroded by consumerism and Western ideology, which is much more individualistic. Shaming people into following traditional mores only works in a nation where most people act in those ways.

Taoism

'Tao is a mystery.
This is the gateway to understanding.'

Lao Tzu, *Tao Te Ching*

FIRST STEPS

The roots of Taoism go back into ancient Chinese culture and folklore. It is a complex amalgam of traditions. By 300 BCE, the text *Tao Te Ching* was in existence, though it is claimed that this dates back to the sixth century BCE. *Tao Te Ching* means 'The Classic Text of the Way of Virtue'. It is ascribed to one Lao Tzu, the 'Old Master'. He was Li Erh Tan, and he is said to have written the text in one night when he was travelling though the mountains. Then he journeyed on into the West, probably a euphemism for dying. It is not certain if there ever was an historical individual, Lao Tzu, but Taoists revere him as the Supreme Immortal. An immortal is a human being who becomes heavenly by virtue, by personal enlightenment.

The *Tao* is a mystical, immanent force that gives life and harmony. It can also be translated as 'the Way'. Trying to define it is like trying to catch hold of flowing water.

Taoism developed in the early centuries CE when two schools joined together, the Way of Heavenly Masters and the Way of Great Peace. A recognized collection or canon of writings and basic precepts was worked out during the *Han* and *T'ang* dynasties.

THE GOAL

The Taoist goal is to live in harmony with the *Tao*, to seek to live at one with nature and to find a stable social order as a result. Ambition and lust for power are wrong as they disrupt this harmony and this flow. Lao Tzu compares the skill of catching and cooking a small fish with ruling a country, for example. Balance, and harmony with the life energy that flows through all living things, the *ch'i*, are the order of the day.

TEACHERS OF THE WAY

Besides the *Tao Te Ching*, Taoists have the *Chuang-Tzu*, written between 369 and 286 BCE. This is even more mystical than the *Tao Te Ching*, focusing on the *Tao* within one's self and how to be in tune with this.

The *I Ching* is also influential, the 'Classic of Changes' manual, which is really a manual of divination. This predated classical Taoism and can also be used by Confucianism.

Flowing water cannot be held, just as the Tao cannot be caught by the mind.

TREASURY OF THE HEART

The Taoist aims to live a long and peaceful life. Longevity is sought through living in harmony with the *Tao* and channelling the life energy – the *ch'i* – properly, through study, right action, diet and exercise. The *Yin/Yang* principle is used as a balance between the five powers of the *ch'i*: wood, fire, earth, metal and water.

PATHS TO PEACE

Taoists have developed exercises of the body and mind, meditation and visualization, called *qigong*. These involve physical posture, breathing and mental disciplines. Visualization imagines deities at different parts of the body, or heavenly light. Taoists follow the Five Precepts:
1. Do not kill.
2. Do not drink alcohol.
3. Do not lie.
4. Do not steal.
5. Do not commit adultery.

Lao Tzu on his final journey east.

There are also the Seven Virtues:
1. Filial piety
2. Loyalty to the emperor
3. Loyalty to teachers
4. Kindness to all creatures
5. Respect for nature
6. Study of sacred texts
7. Offering to the gods.

AWE AND WONDER

Taoists chant, study and meditate, gathered around temples or monasteries. They practise rituals to offer gifts such as incense sticks to the gods.

JOURNEY INTO MYSTERY

Taoists have initiation rites for monks and respect teachers who are wise Masters and adept at meditation exercises. They follow the *Tao* that cannot be understood or described for it cannot be contained or controlled. It is mysterious, like life itself.

Another principle is *Wu-Wei*. This means 'non-action', 'passivity', 'letting be' or 'going with the flow'. It is a way of trying to live in harmony as far as possible and treasuring the simple things of life. It is about being content and changing only what we can.

MAKING MERRY

Taoists have many gods. The old Chinese religion was full of deities, especially household deities and the ancestors. Temples honour some of these, and there are many rituals and festivals for each one. Three main figures emerge from the sea of gods which are all probably aspects of Lao Tzu as the Supreme Immortal: the 'August Old Ruler', the 'August Ruler of the Tao' and the 'Jade Emperor Lord on High'.

Winter sees a renewal festival to maintain the flow of the seasons and the balance of nature.

TODAY

Taoism was persecuted in Communist China until 1976 with the end of the Cultural Revolution. Temples and monasteries were reopened and gods were replaced within them. Taoism is now tolerated as a venerable part of ancient Chinese culture.

In the West, Taoist works are very popular in the New Age movement with their mystical leanings and respect for the environment. The stress on unity and the coherence of all things appeals to modern ears. *Qigong* exercises and disciplines such as *feng shui* derive, in part, from Taoist principles.

Shinto

FIRST STEPS

No one knows the origin of Shinto beliefs. There are no founders, only some legends in an age-old system of folk belief. For example, legends speak of the establishment of the imperial line of emperors in Japan from the sun goddess Amaterasu.

A floating gate at a Shinto shrine.

THE GOAL

Shinto is 'the way of the *kami*', often translated 'gods'. The *kami* are more than gods in the traditional sense. They can be spiritual beings or enlightened humans who have become immortal (such as the teacher Sugawara Michizane who became the *kami* Tenjin). More often than not, they are the symbols of something more impersonal, such as the awe-inspiring beauty of nature. Places of natural beauty in Japan often have shrines and images of the *kami*. Perhaps we should translate the term, 'The Way of the Awesome'.

Worshippers seek blessings and favours from the *kami*. Many students, for example, will visit the *kami* Tenjin for help with examinations.

Shinto does not deal with the afterlife, and so Buddhist rituals take over there.

TEACHERS OF THE WAY

There are no sacred Scriptures as such, but the eighth-century *Nihongi* and the *Kojiki* contain many legends about the creation of the islands and the divinity of the emperor as an example of living *kami, ikigami*. The present rulers of Japan have renounced this claim, though it once was widely held. Some new religious movements that are derived from Shinto do still teach this, however.

TREASURY OF THE HEART

Honouring the *kami* is believed to bring good fortune, and besides the many wayside shrines, there can be household shrines for the protection of the home.

PATHS TO PEACE

Worshippers visit and honour the *kami* by placing a small offering in the collection box. Then they clap twice to alert the *kami* to their presence. They bow twice in respect, recite a short prayer, then bow twice again and depart.

AWE AND WONDER

After paying their respects and offering their petitions, worshippers might leave tokens of this. These are small tablets called *ema*, which are hung around the shrine. Many are about health, success in business or education. Notable exceptions include expressions of sorrow and regret to the spirit of a miscarried child.

JOURNEY INTO MYSTERY

When entering a shrine, believers are entering sacred space. They have to perform purification rites before approaching the *kami*. They will wash out their mouths and wash their hands.

MAKING MERRY

Most acts of prayer are personal. Communal worship takes place at shrine festivals, which usually occur once a year in each village and town. People gather from the local community to form a procession from the shrine around the neighbourhood. The young men carry a portable shrine to transport the blessing of the *kami* around the area.

Besides these, there are rituals at New Year, rice-planting time and harvest.

TODAY

Secularization is a challenge to Shinto. Many Japanese say that they do not believe in the *kami*, but attendance at shrines is still large. It is to be noted that

◆ When did it begin?
   Confucianism - sixth to fifth centuries BCE in China.
   Taoism - sixth century BCE.
   Shinto - ancient faith of Japan.

◆ The founder
   Confucianism - Confucius, or K'ung-fu-Tzu (551–479 CE).
   Taoism - Li Erh Tan (Lao Tzu).
   Shinto - no founders.

◆ God
   Confucianism - agnostic about the gods. Appealed to 'heaven' as an authority.
   Taoism - Many gods, but the *Tao* is a mystical force within all life.
   Shinto - the *kami* gods, exalted saints and spirit beings.

◆ Redeemer – These faiths see no need for a redeemer. Confucianism teaches self-improvement; Taoism appeals for harmony with the *Tao*; Shinto seeks blessing from the gods.

◆ Scriptures
   Confucianism – The *Analects* collect sayings of Confucius.
   Taoism – *Tao Te Ching* of Lao Tzu.
   Shinto – no scriptures but many traditions and stories

◆ Beliefs
   Confucianism – Live in social harmony and nature will follow suit; the true nobleman is one in character, following *jen* and *li*.
   Taoism – Live in harmony with nature (through the *Tao*) to find peace in society.
   Shinto – Seek blessings from the *kami*.

◆ Place of Worship – Taoists have monasteries and temples, and Shinto has numerous shrines.

◆ Sacred Food – Blessing of the rice planting and harvest is important in Shinto.

◆ Main Festivals – Taoism has many festivals to honour the gods, as well as a winter festival. Shinto has festivals to mark the seasons at New Year, spring and autumn.

◆ Key Symbols – The *Yin/Yang* symbol for Confucians and Taoists, suggesting balance and harmony.

many young people leave *ema* behind. Companies often have roof shrines for their employees, and petitions are made for the blessing of new cars, as an example of integrating modern technology with religion.

Shinto is a Japanese phenomenon, and it only travels around the world with Japanese communities. Some new religious movements that derive from Shinto have made some Western converts, such as the *Mahikari* ('True Light') which has a hall in London, England.

One of the more significant derivations from Shinto is Tenrikyo ('religion of heavenly wisdom'). This began in 1838 when a farmer's wife, Nakayama Miki, claimed to be possessed by the spirit of the true Creator of the world, *Tenri Ono Mikoto*. He is said to have chosen Nakayama to guide people to his kingdom of *yokigurashi* ('joyous and blissful life'). It now has about 3 million followers, 1 million of them outside Japan.

JAINISM

'A bird, I have been seized by hawks or trapped in nets, an infinite number of times I have been killed and scraped, split and gutted.'

Uttaradhyayana Sutra

> 'A tree, with axes and adzes by the carpenters an infinite number of times, I have been felled, stripped of my bark, cut up, and sawn into planks...'
>
> **Uttaradhyayana Sutra**
>
> ✳

FIRST STEPS

Varadhamana Mahavira lived from 599–527 BCE and taught in the regions of what is now known as Bihar and Uttar Pradesh. He was the son of a feudal chief and he renounced his life of luxury at the age of 30. He lived as a strict ascetic, abandoning even clothes for the body, to work off the negative karma which he carried. At the age of 42 he claimed to have found enlightenment. He went on teaching for another 30 years until he allowed himself to die by *sallekhana*, a rite of self-starvation. He was known as a 'Jina', one who has conquered 'attachment', and as a 'kevalin', a 'perfected soul'.

THE GOAL

A Jain's goal is not God but enlightenment and freedom from rebirth (*moksha*). Here the soul lives in perfect bliss for eternity, escaping *samsara*, the endless round of rebirths. Jainism is not theistic; there is no sense of a personal God or even a Supreme Being who is the prime mover. Jains take a cyclic view of history, believing that the universe follows an eternal pattern of rise and fall.

TEACHERS OF THE WAY

Mahavira believed that he was the last of 24 Tirthankaras (a synonym for Jinas) or 'Ford Makers' who are the great teachers of Jainism from the end of the third age until the end of the fourth. The fifth began with the death of Mahavira. The Tirthankara before Mahavira was Parsva, who lived 250 years before him.

Jain monks and scholars have kept the original teachings intact though adding commentaries in the Middle Ages. There was a major schism in the first century CE between the Svetambaras and the Digambaras. The main point of contention was over how the monk should dress. The former group wear white robes but the latter maintain the pristine pattern of their founder, going about naked.

TREASURY OF THE HEART

Jains believe that all material things have souls, not just humans, animals and insects. A flame is a fire being that springs into life however briefly. Water and air also contain living souls, as does a stone. These trapped souls have to work out their karma until they are freed and reborn. Jains take a materialistic view of the world, believing each soul to be finite and of definite dimensions. Karma is also understood as a physical force and not just a principle. It is a cloud that lies over the soul, preventing its flying to freedom.

PATHS TO PEACE

Jain monks and nuns follow a stricter code than laymen, brushing the ground before them to avoid taking the lives of insects inadvertently. They have a cloth over their mouths to protect souls in the air, and water has to be strained to protect small creatures. Monks and nuns cannot wash, as this would harm water and the microbes on their bodies. They cannot light or put out a fire, and the monasteries are in total darkness at night.

Laypeople, monks and nuns all have to follow a strict vegetarian diet, though, and laypeople are prohibited from working in certain professions. A farmer would damage the earth and the insects there by ploughing while crafts cause great suffering to the souls in metals, stone and the earth. Laypeople tend to work in commerce.

The Five Principles of Jainism

♦ Avoidance of harm (*Ahimsa*)

♦ Truthfulness (*Satya*)

♦ Non-stealing (*Asteya*)

♦ Chastity (*Brahmacharya*)

♦ Detachment from material things (*Aparigraha*)

AWE AND WONDER

Worship for a Jain involves meditation techniques, the reading or chanting of the Sutras of Mahavira, and honouring of the Tirthankaras in the shrines. The Tirthankaras cannot bless or answer prayers though as they are totally detached from the earth and mortals now. Some forms of Jainism include the Hindu deities in their shrines, but they are seen as lesser beings than the great Tirthankaras. They are not eternal but are more enlightened and can bestow temporary blessings.

JOURNEY INTO MYSTERY

Jainism has a striking story of the progress of the six ages. The first one was sublime, blissful and peaceful when there was no need for morals or teachers. There were 'wishing trees' (*kalpavrksha*) all over the world, providing for people's needs, which gradually withered as things degenerated. Elders were then looked to for guidance before the need arose for the first of the great Tirthankaras.

The endless repetition of these ages seems deterministic but individual souls can seek, through their own free will, to escape the cycle by becoming enlightened.

MAKING MERRY

Jains have the village of Pava, where Mahavira died, as a place of pilgrimage. Their festivals revolve around the cycle of new moons, and monks and nuns always observe a strict fast of *posadha* at this time. Laypeople are invited to join them but most only do so once a year in August. There is a day of penitence and confession of sins called *Paryushana*, followed by a day of rejoicing.

TODAY

There are about four million Jains worldwide, most of whom live in India. Jains have a greater influence than their numbers would suggest, through their hard work and the wealth they earn through business. They often give to hospitals and schools and are active in charitable works. Many Jains are prominent members of the Indian business community.

A Jain holy man sweeps the ground in front of him so that he does not step on any living thing.

Fact Finder

Adonai Hebrew for 'Lord'.

Ahimsa the concept of non-violence.

Ahriman the evil power in Zoroastrianism.

Ahura Mazda 'Wise Lord' or God in Zoroastrianism.

Allah Arabic for God.

Amidah the Jewish prayer said in the morning and evening.

Amrit a mixture of sugar and water used for the initiation of committed Sikhs.

Amritsar the chief city of Sikhism.

Anatman the Buddhist idea of 'no soul' or impermanence.

Apostle 'one who is sent out'.

Ark a container for the scrolls of the Torah in Judaism.

Atman the self or spirit within people, according to Hinduism.

Atonement covering over sins and making peace with God.

Aum or Om; a sacred syllable in Hinduism.

Avatar appearances of the Hindu gods on earth.

Baisakhi (or Vaisakhi) Sikh New Year festival.

Baptism initiation ceremony in Christianity.

Bar-Mitzvah coming-of-age ceremony for Jewish boys.

Bhagavad Gita Hindu Scriptures meaning 'the Song of the Lord'.

Bhakti Hindu path to union with God.

Bible the Christian Scriptures.

Bimah the raised platform in a Jewish synagogue from which the *Torah* is read.

Bismillah 'In the name of Allah', a Muslim prayer.

Bodhisattvas enlightened Buddhist men and women.

Brahman Hindu term for the transcendent godhead.

Buddha 'Enlightened One'.

Caliphs leaders of the Muslim community until modern times.

Ch'i life energy in Chinese thought.

Christ Greek for 'the anointed one'.

Creed statement of belief.

Christmas festival celebrating the birth of Christ.

Chrismation the Eastern Orthodox Christian practice of anointing the newly baptized with oil.

Church The community of all Christians. Also a building used for Christian worship.

Confirmation Western Christian practice in which a bishop lays hands upon a person to confirm their faith.

Dalit one of the lowest castes in Indian society, 'the Untouchables'.

Darshana visiting the deity in the temple in Hindu worship.

Dhammapada early Buddhist text thought to contain many sayings of the Buddha.

Dharma 'Way' or 'Law' or 'Duty' in Hinduism and Buddhism.

Divali Hindu festival of light.

Du'a spontaneous Muslim prayers.

Dukkha Buddhist term for suffering.

Easter festival marking the death and resurrection of Jesus.

Ecumenical a movement to unite Christian denominations.

El or Elohim Jewish term for God.

Eucharist the Holy Communion in Christianity.

Fatwa In Islam, an authoritative declaration.

Five Pillars of Islam The five duties enjoined on every Muslim.

Five Precepts The five ethical restraints for Buddhists.

Four Noble Truths A four-stage summary of the Buddha's teaching.

Ganesha The Hindu elephant god of good beginnings.

Gathas the Zoroastrian Scriptures.

Good Friday Holy day on which Christians remember the crucifixion of Jesus Christ.

Gospel 'good news'; one of four books of the Bible that tell the story of Jesus.

Grace the undeserved favour of God in Christianity.

Granthi a Sikh who recites the *Granth* in Sikh worship.

Gurbani Guru Nanak's teaching.

Gurdwara a Sikh temple.

Gurpurbs Sikh festivals.

Guru Indian teacher.

Guru Granth Sahib Sikh holy book.

Hadith teachings of Muhammad and the prophets.

Hajj pilgrimage to Makkah in Islam.

Hanifs seekers after the one God in Arabia in pre-Islamic times.

Hannukah eight-day Jewish festival.

Haoma plant used for a sacramental drink in Zoroastrianism.

Heaven the realm of God or of the gods.

Hell The realm where the wicked go after death.

Holi a Hindu spring festival.

Holy Spirit third person of the Christian Trinity.

Hukan Sikh practice of opening the *Granth* and placing the finger on a verse to find guidance.

Icon a holy image of Christ or the saints in Eastern Christianity.

Id-ul-Adha Muslim festival marking the end of Hajj.

Id-ul-Fitr The Muslim festival which ends the fasting of Ramadan.

Imam Types of leader within Islam.

Incarnation the Christian belief that God became man in Jesus.

ISKON the International Society for Krishna Consciousness, a Hindu movement.